Soaring Without Limits

A Guide to Elevating Your Thoughts and Transforming Your Life

MONIQUE S. PEARSON

Copyright © 2024 by Monique S. Pearson

All Rights Reserved. Except as permitted under the U.S. Copyright Act of 1976, no part of this publication may be reproduced, distributed, or transmitted in any form or by any means or stored in a database or retrieval system without the prior written permission of the publisher.

Any unauthorized copying, translation, duplication, importation, or distribution, in whole or in part, by any means, including electronic copying, storage, or transmission, is a violation of applicable laws.

Table of Contents

Disclaimer vii
Forward ix
Introduction xi

SECTION1: ELEVATE

1. It's Time to "Elevate"! 1
2. Self Awareness 4
   What is Self-Awareness? 5
   Recognizing and Enhancing Self-Awareness 5
   Building Self-Awareness 6
   The Impostor in the Mirror 7
   Key Characteristics of Impostor Syndrome 7
   A Self-Assessment Exercise 9
   Summing It Up 10
   Reflection Questions 10
3. Thinking Traps 12
   What are Thinking Traps? 13
   Overcoming Thinking Traps 15
   Summing It Up 16
   Reflection Questions 17
4. Positive Affirmations 18
   What Are Affirmations? 19

    Why Affirmations Are Your New Best Friend..20
    Affirmation Station: How to Make It Happen 20
    Create Your Own Affirmation Magic 21
    Summing It Up 22
    Reflection Questions...22

5. **Daily Gratitude**..23
    The Power of Perspective: Understanding Gratitude...............................24
    The Ripple Effect...25
    Exercises to Cultivate Thankfulness...26
    Summing It Up 27
    Reflection Questions..28

6. **SMART Goals**..29
    The SMART Way 30
    Why SMART Goals Work...32
    Your Turn to Set SMART Goals..32
    Summing It Up 35
    Reflection Questions..36

7. **Moving on "Elevate"** 37
    Key Concepts: The Pillars of "Elevate"..38
    Actionable Steps 39
    Expanding Your Horizons: What's Next? 40

SESSION 2: EXPAND

8. **From Elevation to Expansion**..42

9. **Limited Self-Beliefs and Self-Imposed Limitations** 46
    Defining Limited Self-Beliefs and Self-Imposed Limitations 48
    Uncovering My Roots of Limitation 50
    The Theory Behind Limited Self-Beliefs and Self-Imposed Limitations. 51

    Practices to Battle Limited Self-Beliefs and Self-Imposed Limitations ... 52
    Practice Visualization 53

10. How Not to Fear Failure..54
    Defining Failure.. 55
    Practices to Battle Fear of Failure 56
    My Journey Continues... 56
    Summing It Up 58
    Reflection Questions.. 58

11. Embrace New Experiences, Challenges, and Step Out of Your Comfort Zone 59
    How Embracing New Challenges Helps You Grow Personally and Professionally 61
    From Panic to Possibility 63
    Tips for Embracing New Experiences 64
    Summing It Up: 65
    Reflection Questions.. 67

12. Surround Yourself with Supportive and Uplifting Individuals Who Encourage Personal Growth 68
    How Positive People Impact Your View of Yourself and the World........ 70
    How to Find Good People to Surround Yourself With 71
    How to Release Negative People 72
    Summing It Up 72
    Reflection Questions.. 73

13. Moving on to "Explore" 74
    Key Concepts: The Pillars of "Expand" 75
    Actionable Steps 75
    Exploring New Depths: What's Next? 76

SESSION 3: EXPLORE

14. From Expansion to Exploration 79

15. Showing Yourself Grace and Compassion 83
Understanding Mindfulness: A Path to Self-Awareness 84
Twenty Years of Silence 86
Practicing Self-Compassion..87
Practicing Self-Care 89
Summing It Up 91
Reflection Questions..92

16. Implementing and Maintaining Daily Spiritual Practice 93
Spirituality Theory..94
Ten Days That Tested Everything..97
Reflection Questions.. 101

17. The Power of Exploration 102
Key Concepts: The Pillars of "Explore" 103
Actionable Steps 103
Exploring New Depths: What's Next? 104

Conclusion 106

Resources 109

Disclaimer

The content of this book is based on my personal experiences and insights gained throughout my life journey. While I strive to provide helpful and inspiring information, it's important to note that I am not a trained mental health professional, psychologist, or therapist.

The strategies, advice, and reflections shared in this book are drawn from my own personal growth and should not be considered professional medical or psychological advice. Every individual's situation is unique, and what has worked for me may not be universally applicable.

If you are dealing with mental health issues, trauma, or any serious personal challenges, I strongly encourage you to seek help from qualified professionals. This book is not a substitute for professional therapy, counseling, or medical advice.

Remember, your mental health and well-being are of utmost importance. While personal stories and experiences can be inspiring and insightful, they should complement, not replace, professional guidance when needed.

By reading this book, you acknowledge that the author is sharing personal experiences and perspectives, not professional expertise in mental health or psychology. Always consult with licensed professionals for advice concerning your specific situation.

Thank you for your time, and I hope this journey is as enlightening for you as it was for me.

Forward

∞

In every journey, whether personal or collective, moments challenge the very core of who we are. The path ahead may twist, turn, and, at times, seem impossible to navigate. Yet, it is in these moments that we discover our strength. It is when the road is darkest that courage takes root, and when uncertainty looms, that determination becomes our compass.

To be brave is not to be fearless but to face fear with unwavering resolve. Monique looks at the fear head-on, no matter how fast her heart beats . She makes a plan to stand. Bravery is the ability to forge ahead, no matter the obstacles, no matter the passage. Monique's resilience defines those who rise above circumstance, turn setbacks into stepping stones, and transform challenges into triumphs.

This book stands as a testament to that unyielding spirit—the relentless drive to push forward, to overcome, and to build something greater than oneself. It is a call to those who dare to keep moving when the world says stop and to those who believe that every barrier holds within it the seed of opportunity.

No matter how treacherous the path, our ability to press onward is what shapes our destiny. This is not just a story of survival but of triumph. Let this serve as a reminder: we are all capable of greatness when we choose to rise, persevere, and never back down.

As you read this book, make your plans to forge ahead and to never waver in the moment of what seems to be defeat.

KAREN MCKOY
Resilience Strategist Counselor, Author, Speaker, Artist

Introduction

∞

I was always known as the quiet one, the one who didn't speak but who allowed her actions to speak for her. But underneath that calm exterior, I was dealing with some real stuff. I'm talking extreme shyness, no voice to speak of, rock-bottom self-confidence, and self-esteem so low you'd need a shovel to find it. I second-guessed everything about myself and what I tried to accomplish. For the longest time, I didn't know my power or my worth.

It wasn't until probably my 30s that I started truly finding myself. This transformation didn't happen overnight. It meant facing some hard truths and learning how to move past them.

One of the biggest hurdles I had to overcome was dealing with childhood trauma. At six years old, I experienced child molestation— an event so traumatic that my mind protected me by repressing the memory until I was 16. When the memories resurfaced, I didn't know how to cope. Instead of seeking help, I chose to bury them again, to squelch the pain and pretend it never happened.

But, the thing is, trauma doesn't simply disappear when ignored. You can't hold in over 20 years of various incidents and expect that life can continue to go as normal. It's going to reach a point where it's going to boil over, and it's not going to be pretty.

I learned that the hard way.

I held these experiences in, thinking I could contain them, but the weight of unresolved pain led to self-destructive behaviors. Eventually, everything boils over.

For years, I applied the tools and coping mechanisms that I had learned at a young age in my adulthood. But they were crippling me at this point rather than helping me. Consequently, I had to learn new tools as I was growing and developing as a woman, as what I used as my crutch as a child was no longer serving me . It took therapy, self-reflection, and a whole lot of work to understand what needed to change in order for me to heal from my childhood wounds.

This book is born from that journey. It's a roadmap for those who, like me, have struggled with self-doubt, trauma, or simply feeling lost in their own lives. Through the pages that follow, I'll share the strategies and insights that helped me elevate my thought processes, challenge negative patterns, and ultimately transform my life.

Remember, every individual has a choice to decide whether or not to improve their mindset. Our mindsets are not fixed; there is always an opportunity to embrace growth. All it takes is the decision to do so and the willingness to put in the work.

This is going to be a comprehensive guide designed to help you unlock your full potential and transform your life through mindset shifts and practical strategies. We're going to divide this journey into three main sections: Elevate, Expand, and Explore.

INTRODUCTION

In the "Elevate" section, we're going to learn how to elevate our thought processes and perception of self. I'm going to guide you through techniques to overcome thinking traps, learn how to successfully challenge negative thought patterns, and replace them with positive affirmations. We're going to talk about the importance of gratitude and how to set SMART goals as tools for personal growth.

Moving on to the "Expand" section, we're going to focus on breaking free from those self-imposed limitations and embracing a growth mindset. I'm going to encourage you to step out of your comfort zone, embrace new experiences and challenges, and surround yourself with supportive and uplifting individuals who encourage personal growth. We'll also talk about the importance of showing yourself grace and compassion during this journey.

Finally, in the "Explore" section, we're going to imagine the possibilities that come with this changed mindset. We'll dive into how self-awareness is crucial for initiating change, and I'll encourage you to engage in self-care activities and maintain a consistent spiritual practice.

Throughout the book, I'm going to share personal stories, give you practical exercises, and provide actionable strategies to help you implement these concepts in your daily life. My goal is to empower you to take control of your mindset, overcome past traumas and limitations, and create a life of fulfillment and purpose.

So, are you ready to elevate your thought processes, expand your understanding of your capabilities, and explore how you can shift any thought patterns that are no longer serving you?

Let's get started!

SECTION 1: ELEVATE

1

It's Time to "Elevate"!

"Sometimes what appears to be a setback is God's mode of elevation."
- Roderick L. Evans

∞

Reflecting back, it occurred to me that the origin of my shyness, lack of a voice, low self-confidence, and low self-esteem was trauma. Being molested at 6 years old, I learned how to keep secrets, to shrink so that I may go unnoticed, and to hide in the background. These actions served as my protective armor to protect me from other predators as well as bullies. These tactics may have served me in my childhood to help me feel safe, but they were causing me damage in my adulthood because they prevented me from blooming into the woman God called me to be.

This realization was the first step in my journey of elevation. But what does it mean to "elevate" oneself?

To elevate means to raise to a higher level, to lift up, to improve morally, intellectually, or culturally. In the context of personal growth and mindset transformation, elevation is about raising our thoughts, beliefs, and actions to a level that aligns with our true potential.

In order for one to accomplish feats they have never done before, one has to think in ways they have never done before. One must elevate one's thoughts in order to elevate one's life. This is the core principle of the elevation process. It's about challenging the status quo of our minds, questioning the beliefs that have held us back, and daring to think bigger and bolder than we ever have before.

Throughout this section, we'll explore how you can elevate your thought processes and perception of self. We'll delve into strategies that will help you recognize and reframe negative thought patterns, build self-confidence, and cultivate a more positive self-image.

The lesson I want you to take away from this section is this: Every individual has a choice to decide whether or not to improve his or her mindset. Our mindsets are not fixed. There is an opportunity to embrace a growth mindset; all it takes is a decision to do so. This choice, this decision, is the first step in your elevation journey.

My purpose in sharing this information is to teach you how to begin reprogramming your thought processes. You'll learn actionable steps that you can implement right away to change your mindset, which in turn will change your life for the better. Remember, small shifts in thinking can lead to massive changes in your life outcomes.

In the chapters that follow, we'll focus on several key areas that are crucial to the elevation process. We'll explore self-awareness, which involves learning to truly understand ourselves and our thought patterns. We'll identify and tackle thinking traps that keep us stuck in negative cycles.

IT'S TIME TO "ELEVATE"

We'll harness the power of positive affirmations to rewire our internal dialogue. We'll also cultivate daily gratitude to shift our focus towards the positive aspects of our lives. And we'll learn how to set SMART goals to turn our elevated thinking into tangible results.

This journey of elevation isn't always easy, but it's infinitely worthwhile. As we progress through these chapters, remember that you're not alone. I've walked this path, and I'm here to guide you every step of the way.

2

SELF AWARENESS

∞

I'm going to be real with you for a minute. I was 37 years old when I started my self-improvement journey. You heard that right. *Thirty-seven.* That's when I finally felt ready to start improving myself, going to therapy and engaging in other activities to heal from my childhood and young adulthood trauma.

For years, I was running from myself. I was running away from getting to the roots of my issues, my behaviors, and what caused me to react the way I did and do the things that I did. I was operating in "trauma response mode" because I didn't think I would be strong enough to face everything. So , for all those years, I refused to do any self-reflective work. I continuously stayed busy to fill time so I wouldn't have dead spaces to reflect and look within myself.

Why did it take me so long?

Well, I felt that I wasn't strong enough emotionally to revisit the past. But let me tell you something—that running, that avoiding, was like wearing track shoes all the time. And honestly, those shoes get mighty uncomfortable after a while.

Now, I'm gonna break down self-awareness for you because it's crucial to this whole journey we're on together.

What is Self-Awareness?

According to the *Oxford Dictionary*, self-awareness is a mental state in which the individual is aware of itself as having knowledge about itself (Oxford Reference, n.d.). In other words, it is the ability to understand your own personality, emotions, and thoughts. It involves recognizing your strengths and weaknesses, understanding your values and beliefs, and being aware of your actions and their impact on others (Cherry, 2024). Essentially, it is the capacity to observe and analyze yourself objectively.

Recognizing and Enhancing Self-Awareness

While you may not constantly focus on self-awareness, it becomes crucial in various situations and stages of life. For example, self-awareness helps one navigate decisions, reflect on one's behavior, and interact with others more effectively. By understanding your thoughts and behaviors, you can analyze situations more effectively and make better decisions. Knowing your strengths and areas for improvement helps you build confidence and self-respect. Self-awareness also allows you to see situations from different angles, broadening your understanding and empathy for others. Additionally, being aware of your emotions and motivations leads to more informed and thoughtful choices. Understanding your triggers and habits enables you to manage your reactions and behaviors more effectively.

Now, by definition, having a "lack of self-awareness" means that, well, you are *unaware* that you are *not* aware! To find out if you have low self-awareness, ask yourself these questions:

1. Do you always have to be in control?
2. Do you always have to be the center of attention?
3. Do you make negative comments without a filter?
4. Do you make impulsive decisions?
5. Do you have difficulty taking criticism from others and revert to a defensive posture?

It's important to note that this list is not all-encompassing. These questions are meant to be a starting point for self-reflection, not a comprehensive assessment. Self-awareness is a complex and multifaceted concept, and everyone's journey to self-awareness is unique. To probe further into your level of self-awareness, consider asking yourself additional questions as needed.

"Am I stepping on any toes with this criteria?" If you are, don't worry. The good news is this is an area that can be improved.

Building Self-Awareness

If you identify with any of these signs, don't worry. Self-awareness is a skill that can be developed and improved over time. Now, I know some of you might be thinking, "Monique, that sounds great, but how do I improve my self-awareness?" Well, I've got some tips for you:

Steps to Improve Self Awareness
1. Start journaling to understand your feelings and the motives behind your actions.
2. Practice mindfulness to be in the moment and notice how situations make you feel.
3. Ask your family and friends for feedback on how they view you and how you come across to others.

Now that we've talked about self-awareness, I want to explore something that often arises when we start looking at ourselves honestly: A little thing called impostor syndrome. You might be thinking, "What does that have to do with me?" Well, it has everything to do with all of us.

The Impostor in the Mirror

Do you ever feel like you're just faking it till you make it, but you're not sure you'll ever really make it? That's impostor syndrome.

Impostor syndrome, also known as impostor phenomenon, is a pervasive issue that affects many high-achieving individuals. The *Oxford Dictionary* defines impostor syndrome as " persistent inability to believe that one's success is not deserved or has not been legitimately achieved as a result of one's own efforts or skills" (Oxford English Dictionary. (n.d.).

Characterized by chronic self-doubt and a sense of intellectual fraudulence, those experiencing impostor syndrome feel as though they are undeserving of their accomplishments despite clear evidence of their competence and success (Huecker, 2023). In more simple terms, impostor syndrome means that you're pretending that everything is okay. Everyone sees you on social media and thinks that all is well with you, but on the inside, you're silently screaming. You're crying for help because you know that the person you're portraying is not your true self.

Key Characteristics of Impostor Syndrome

This section will explain the main traits of impostor syndrome, helping you recognize and understand how it affects those who experience it (Point Loma Nazarene University, n.d.).

> **Key Characteristics of Impostor Syndrome**
>
> 1. Impostor Cycle: This cycle begins with either over-preparation or procrastination, driven by a fear of failure. Even after you complete the task, any success you achieve feels fleeting, and you may quickly slide back into feelings of inadequacy, keeping the cycle going.
> 2. Perfectionism: You might set impossibly high standards for yourself, driven by the need to be the best. This relentless pursuit of perfection can lead to harsh self-criticism, burnout, and a refusal to recognize your own achievements.
> 3. Super-Heroism: To counteract feelings of inadequacy, you might over-prepare for tasks to appear exceptionally capable. While this can temporarily ease feelings of fraudulence, it often results in mental exhaustion and reinforces the impostor cycle.
> 4. Atychiphobia: You may worry that any mistake will reveal you as a fraud, leading to intense anxiety and avoidance of risk-taking.
> 5. Achievemephobia: Also called "the fear of success," this can be just as paralyzing as the fear of failure. You might be apprehensive that success will bring higher expectations and more pressure, causing you to downplay or minimize your achievements.

Now that we've pulled back the curtain on impostor syndrome, you might be feeling a little exposed. Maybe you're nodding your head, thinking, "Yep, that's me." Or maybe you're not sure where you stand. Either way, it's time to dig a little deeper. You see, understanding impostor syndrome is one thing, but figuring out how it applies to you personally? That's where the real work begins.

A Self-Assessment Exercise

Now, we're going to do a little self-assessment exercise. Don't worry; this isn't some test you can fail. It's all about understanding yourself better. This exercise will help you sit back and assess how you view yourself and actually give yourself a ranking as to your self-**confidence** and your perception of self. That's powerful stuff. And here's a tough question: Would *you* recommend *yourself* to someone else?

Follow these Steps:

1. Find a quiet space where you won't be disturbed for about 30 minutes.
2. Grab a pen and paper, or open up a notes app on your phone.
3. Take a few deep breaths to center yourself.
4. Now, rate yourself on a scale of 1-10 (1 being the lowest, 10 being the highest) on the following:
   - Your overall self-confidence
   - How much you like yourself
   - Your ability to achieve your goals
   - How well you handle criticism
   - Your comfort level in social situations
5. Write down three words that describe how you see yourself.
6. List three things you're proud of about yourself.
7. List three areas where you feel you need improvement.
8. Finally, answer this question honestly: If you met someone exactly like you, would you recommend them to a friend or employer? Why or why not?

Now, let's talk about what all this means. If you've given yourself mostly high scores and can easily list things you're proud of, that's fantastic! You've got a strong foundation of self-confidence to build on. But if you're seeing a lot of low scores or struggling to find things you like about yourself, don't worry. This is just your starting point, and recognizing it is the first step to making positive changes.

Remember, there's no "perfect" score here. We all have areas where we feel more or less confident. The goal of this exercise is to give you a clearer picture of how you see yourself right now. It's about awareness, not judgment. And here's the beautiful thing: if you don't like what you see, you have the power to change it. This is the beginning of your journey to a more confident, self-aware you.

Summing It Up

In this chapter, we looked at how impostor syndrome can weaken your confidence and success by twisting your self-view. Recognizing its main traits can help you see how it affects your growth both personally and professionally.

In the next chapter, we'll explore thinking traps.

Reflection Questions

1. What does your ideal self look like?
2. What are your dreams/goals?
3. What is keeping you from your dreams/goals?
4. Rank the top ten most important things in your life. (Career, family, relationships, etc.)

5. How much time do you dedicate to each of these things?
6. Would you recommend it to others?
7. Describe yourself in three words .
8. What qualities do you most admire in yourself?
9. What things scare you?
10. Ask yourself: Do you treat yourself better than others?

3

Thinking Traps

∞

We've already explored impostor syndrome and how it can smash your confidence and make you second-guess your achievements. However, impostor syndrome is just one part of the puzzle. In this chapter, we will discuss a different but equally important aspect of how our minds can work against us: thinking traps.

Have you ever found yourself second-guessing your abilities or feeling like you're not good enough, even when you've achieved something great? Maybe you compare yourself to others, thinking that you don't truly belong or deserve your success.

If the answer is yes, let me share something from a class I took on thinking traps as part of the "Comprehensive Soldier and Family Fitness" Master Resilience Training. This was a joint initiative between the U.S. Army and the University of Pennsylvania, and it was completely eye-opening. I found it incredibly valuable because the training revealed how our thoughts could trip us up without us even realizing it. Within this seminar, I learned about thinking traps.

Thinking traps are common patterns of unproductive or negative thinking that distort how we see situations and reinforce feelings of inadequacy.

THINKING TRAPS

Imagine wearing blinders— not to block your view but to cloud your ability to think clearly. Unlike impostor syndrome, which centers on doubting your worthiness despite evidence of success, thinking traps are broader cognitive distortions that affect how you view yourself and your situations overall.

We'll break down these thinking traps, exploring how they operate and why they can be so damaging. I'll share insights from the resilience training class I took, which shed light on these patterns and their impact. We'll cover six main thinking traps, look at expert perspectives, and discuss practical strategies to overcome them.

Understanding and addressing these thinking traps will not only help you tackle impostor syndrome more effectively but also improve your overall self-awareness and confidence. Ready to uncover and combat these mental pitfalls? Here we go.

What are Thinking Traps?

You know, it's easy to fall into these patterns without even realizing it. We're all humans, and our brains sometimes take shortcuts that don't always serve us well. But the good news is, once we can spot these traps, we can learn to sidestep them. Let me break it down for you with some real-life examples:

Types of Thinking Traps		
Thinking Trap	**Definition**	*Example*
Jumping to Conclusions	This is when we think we know for sure what's going on, even though we don't have much evidence.	Imagine you text your friend, and they don't respond for hours. You might jump to the conclusion that they're

	Types of Thinking Traps	
		mad at you or ignoring you on purpose. But in reality, they could be in a meeting, their phone could be dead, or they might just be taking a nap.
Mind Reading	This is when we assume we know what someone else is thinking, or we expect them to know what's going on in our head.	Your boss gives you a new project, and you think, "She must not trust me with the big clients." But maybe she's actually giving you this project because she thinks you're ready for more responsibility.
Me, Me, Me	This is when we take on all the responsibility for every problem we run into.	Your team misses a deadline at work, and you immediately think, "This is all my fault. I should have worked harder." But in reality, there were probably many factors that contributed to missing the deadline.
Them, Them, Them	This is the opposite: blaming everyone else for our problems.	You're late to an important meeting, and you think, "If only the traffic wasn't so bad, if only my alarm clock worked properly, if only my coffee maker didn't break this morning."

Types of Thinking Traps		
		You're blaming everything and everyone but yourself.
Always, Always, Always	This is when we think negative things are never going to change, and we can't do anything about it.	You struggle with public speaking and think, "I'll always be terrible at presentations. I'll never improve no matter how much I practice."
Everything, Everything, Everything	This is when we judge our whole worth based on one event, or we think one problem is going to mess up our entire life.	You make a mistake at work and think, "I'm a complete failure. I'm going to get fired, and I'll never find another job. My whole career is ruined."

See how easy it is to fall into these traps? Recognizing them is the first step to overcoming them. In the next section, we'll talk about how to challenge these thoughts and replace them with more balanced, realistic thinking. Remember, we're not aiming for perfection here. We're just trying to be a little bit better each day at catching these traps before they catch us.

Overcoming Thinking Traps

You might be wondering, "This all sounds great, but how do I actually put it into practice?" That's where the strategies come in. Each thinking trap has a specific approach to counter it:

For "Jumping to Conclusions ," the key is to slow down and actively seek out evidence before making judgments. This helps ensure that you're not basing decisions on incomplete information.

For "Mind Reading ," the solution is to communicate openly. Instead of assuming you know what others are thinking, ask questions to clarify their thoughts and intentions.

With "Me, Me, Me ," shift your focus outward. Evaluate how external factors or other people might have influenced the situation rather than taking all the responsibility on yourself.

In the case of "Them, Them, Them ," turn the lens inward. Reflect on your own actions and consider how you might have contributed to the issue at hand.

For "Always, Always, Always ," take charge by identifying aspects you can change. Instead of believing that negative situations will never improve, focus on what is within your control.

When dealing with "Everything, Everything, Everything ," get specific. Break down the situation to understand what's really happening rather than letting one event overshadow your entire perspective.

Now, take a moment to reflect on your own experiences. Can you identify times when you've fallen into these traps? It's completely normal to do so; we all encounter these patterns. The goal is to recognize them and work on shifting your thinking.

Summing It Up

Remember, the goal here isn't to beat ourselves up for having these thoughts. It's about building our resilience. By learning to spot these traps and fighting back against them, we're working on our self-awareness, our self-regulation, our optimism, and our mental agility. We're building our character strengths and improving our connections with others.

As we move into the next chapter, I want you to keep these thinking traps in mind. We're going to be talking about positive affirmations, and understanding these traps will help you see why affirmations can be so powerful. They're not just feel-good statements - they're tools to help us fight back against these counterproductive thoughts that can hold us back.

Reflection Questions

1. Can you recall a recent situation where you felt stuck in one of the thinking traps? Which trap were you experiencing (e.g., Jumping to Conclusions, Mind Reading)?
2. When you found yourself jumping to conclusions, what evidence did you have (or lack) to support your initial thoughts?
3. Have there been times when you assumed you knew what someone else was thinking? How accurate were your assumptions?
4. Reflect on a time when you took excessive responsibility for a problem. What other factors or people might have contributed to the issue?
5. Think of an instance where you blamed others for a problem. What role did you play in the situation?
6. What steps can you take to acknowledge your part and address any underlying issues more constructively?
7. Have you ever felt trapped by the belief that negative circumstances will never improve? What aspects of the situation were within your control?
8. How can focusing on what you can change help you manage feelings of helplessness or frustration?
9. Can you identify a time when you judged your entire worth based on a single event? What was the actual impact of that event on your overall life?
10. What strategies have you found most effective in addressing these thinking traps? How have they impacted your self-awareness and resilience?

4

POSITIVE AFFIRMATIONS

∞

Now that we understand thinking traps, it's time to dive into the power of positive affirmations and how they can transform your life, just like they did mine. For me, it all started when I was willing to start doing the work at 37. When I looked at myself in the mirror, I noticed that my self-talk was not the best. There was a lot of negative self-talk. To improve myself, I started practicing these daily affirmations.

So, I came up with a list of things that I wanted to change in my life. I got a paper, and on one side of the paper, I wrote down all of that negative self-talk that I had. Then, on the other side, I wrote down the opposite of what I wanted that to be. Every morning, I'd hop in the shower and start talking aloud about everything I wanted myself to be that I wasn't. In fact, I repeated my affirmations three times a day. I continued to do that until I noticed that everything that I came up with came to fruition.

In this way, I learned that I actually *could* speak things into existence. I pretty much reprogramed my subconscious to bring to my conscious and reality those things I desired to see. Now, 11 years later, it's still a part of my daily routine. As I accomplish things, I revise my affirmations, always pushing myself to grow.

What Are Affirmations?

Positive affirmations can help people better respond to challenging messages. Research has proven that affirming core values can help us improve our mental state and our lives altogether. For example, a study found that when people thought about their core values before receiving health advice, they were more open to the messages and changed their behavior.

In the study, participants engaged in a self-affirmation exercise, reflecting on their core values before being exposed to health messages encouraging more physical activity. Results revealed that those who practiced self-affirmation showed increased activity in the ventromedial prefrontal cortex (VMPFC), which is a brain region associated with self-related processing and positive thinking. This increase in brain activity was connected to greater reductions in sedentary behavior over the next month (Falk et al., 2015). In other words, self-affirmation makes health messages seem more relevant and less threatening, which helps people make positive changes.

In summary, self-affirmation enhances how we receive and respond to challenging information, offering a promising approach to improving health behaviors and other interventions. Affirmations aren't just feel-good statements. They're powerful tools for reshaping your mindset. Basically, the purpose of affirmations is to erase and improve your self-perception and to eradicate negative thoughts. They work by consistently reinforcing positive beliefs about yourself, which, over time, can change your subconscious patterns of thinking.

Why Affirmations Are Your New Best Friend

You might be wondering why I repeat my affirmations three times a day. Well, it's all about consistency and reinforcement. By repeating your affirmations regularly, you're essentially rewiring your brain. It's like exercising a muscle ; the more you do it, the stronger it gets.

Let me break down why affirmations are so powerful:

1. They challenge negative self-talk
2. They boost self-confidence
3. They help you visualize and believe in your goals
4. They can reduce stress and anxiety
5. They promote a more positive outlook on life

Embracing affirmations can lead to profound changes in your self-talk, confidence, and overall outlook. By challenging negative thoughts, boosting self-esteem, and promoting a positive mindset, affirmations become a tool for growth and resilience. Now that you understand their power, let's explore how to make affirmations a practical part of your daily routine.

Affirmation Station: How to Make It Happen

Now that you see the value in affirmations, it's time to put them into practice. Creating effective affirmations is about making them personal and meaningful, ensuring they align with your goals and values. Here's how to tailor them for maximum impact.

1. Make them personal: Your affirmations should resonate with you. Don't just copy someone else's.
2. Keep them in present tense: Say "I am," not "I will be."

3. Make them positive: Focus on what you want, not what you don't want.
4. Repeat them regularly: I'm talking at least three times a day, folks.
5. Feel them: Don't just say the words; really feel their truth.

Crafting personalized affirmations that resonate with you is key to their effectiveness. By making them specific, positive, and emotionally engaging, you'll reinforce your goals and boost your self-belief. With this foundation in place, let's dive into creating your own affirmation magic and tailoring them to fit your unique journey.

Create Your Own Affirmation Magic

When giving training on this, I typically give examples of the types of affirmations that I have used over the years that I have found helpful. I've even made an affirmation mantra that I've said every morning for years until each one came to fruition.

But here's the thing: I believe everyone needs to make it personal to them. When you give people examples, they'll often take your examples versus trying to come up with what's applicable to them. That's why I h ave come up with additional ways for others t o create their own positive affirmations. I call them thought prompts .

Taking this into consideration, here are some prompts to get you started as you begin your own affirmation journey:

1. What negative self-talk do you want to change?
2. What qualities do you admire in others that you want to cultivate in yourself?
3. What goals are you working towards?
4. What makes you feel strong and capable?

Take some time to reflect on these questions and craft affirmations that speak to your heart. Customizing your affirmations allows you to connect more deeply with them, making your practice more effective. Use the prompts provided to reflect on your personal goals and values. By designing affirmations that speak to you, you're setting yourself up for a more empowered and focused journey.

Summing It Up

As we conclude our discussion on affirmations, it's important to consider how to weave this practice seamlessly into your daily routine. Reflecting on your personal experience with affirmations will help you solidify their role in your growth and development.

By evaluating your current self-talk, imagining the impact of affirmations on your mindset, and taking concrete steps to integrate them into your daily life, you lay the groundwork for meaningful and lasting change. Preparing for potential obstacles will ensure that affirmations become a consistent and powerful part of your personal development journey. With this foundation established, let's move forward to explore another transformative practice: daily gratitude.

Reflection Questions

1. What negative self-talk patterns have you noticed in yourself?
2. How do you think daily affirmations could change your mindset?
3. What's one affirmation you can start using today?
4. How can you incorporate affirmations into your daily routine?
5. What potential obstacles might you face in practicing affirmations, and how can you overcome them?

5

Daily Gratitude

∞

Back in 2015, I experienced something that would go on to change my life forever. I was just starting my first business, a multi-level marketing company, while still working a 10-hour day for the government. Even to this day, when I close my eyes, it feels like it just happened yesterday.

Picture this: It was 2:30 in the morning, and I was supposed to meet my cousin to drive to North Carolina for a convention.

I dragged myself out of bed, feeling like a zombie. *I'll just grab an energy drink*, I thought to myself. *That'll do the trick.*

I hopped in the car, ready for the 45-minute drive from Maryland to DC, where my cousin lives.

Next thing I knew, I was waking up with my head on the steering wheel.

The music was still playing, the car was still running, but both front tires were flat. I looked up to see a tree split in half—what had ultimately stopped me. I had jumped the curb, narrowly missed a metal pole, and ended up on a small island in the middle of the road.

In the immediate aftermath, my thoughts were filled with self-blame. I blamed myself for falling asleep, wrecking my car, and causing inconvenience. It was early morning, and I found myself calling my boyfriend for help, arranging a rental car, and informing my cousin that we would be late.

But then it hit me… was I crazy? I could have hit that pole and seriously injured myself or someone else. *But I didn't.*

The only things damaged were the tree and my car, and cars can be replaced. I realized that I was the most valuable thing, and I had narrowly escaped a much worse situation.

That's when I knew that I had to shift my perspective. Instead of focusing on all the negatives, I found gratitude. I was grateful I could walk away unscathed, grateful I didn't hurt anyone else, grateful I could still make it to the conference.

Gratitude, in this way, is a profound and transformative emotion with the power to significantly enhance our well-being. This chapter explores the science behind gratitude, its benefits, and how it can improve our mental, physical, and relational health. By looking closely at various aspects of gratitude, we will uncover how cultivating this practice can lead to a more fulfilling and resilient life.

The Power of Perspective: Understanding Gratitude

You might be wondering, what exactly is gratitude? It's more than just saying "thank you" when someone holds the door open for you. Gratitude is a deeper appreciation for what you have in your life, both the big things and the small.

Positive psychology research has shown that practicing gratitude can significantly enhance our well-being. It essentially trains our minds to focus on the positive aspects of life, even when we face challenges.

Research has demonstrated that gratitude is more than a transient feeling. It supports better health, happiness, and wisdom in both individuals and communities. In fact, the Greater Good Science Center at the University of California, Berkeley, describes gratitude as the "social glue" that strengthens relationships (Pratt, 2022). For instance, research involving nearly 300 university counseling clients found that those who wrote gratitude letters weekly for three weeks experienced better mental health compared to those who did not. Similarly, a study on writing down daily blessings showed that participants felt happier and less depressed six months later (Pratt, 2022).

So, it's clear that gratitude practices enhance emotional resilience and mental well-being. Let's explore how daily gratitude practices can create a ripple effect, leading to long-term improvements in various areas of life.

The Ripple Effect

As I always say, "When you focus on the good, you're opening up that space for more good to come in. And that's programming you to look for the good once you start doing that on a consistent basis as to what you're great at." This leads us to the benefits of daily gratitude.

It's not just about feeling good at the moment. It has some serious long-term benefits:

Benefits of Gratitude
1. It improves your mental health: Gratitude can reduce depression and anxiety.
2. It enhances your physical health: Grateful people tend to take better care of themselves.
3. It strengthens relationships: Expressing gratitude to others can deepen your connections.
4. It increases resilience: When you're grateful, you're better equipped to handle life's challenges.

Ultimately, gratitude's benefits extend beyond momentary happiness. Regular practice can lead to significant improvements in mental health, physical health, relationships, and resilience. Grateful individuals often experience reduced depression, better self-care, stronger relationships, and enhanced ability to handle challenges. This underscores its importance in enhancing overall well-being. The next section will provide practical exercises to help you cultivate and maintain a daily gratitude practice.

Exercises to Cultivate Thankfulness

Incorporating gratitude into daily life requires practical exercises. This section provides actionable strategies to help you develop and sustain a gratitude practice, making it a natural and impactful part of your routine.

I want you to start by making a list of what you're thankful for. Because that's also shifting the directive of focusing on what is going wrong and what is needed to what is going right in your life. Here are some exercises to get you started:

Gratitude Exercises
1. Gratitude Journaling: At the end of each day, reflect and write down three things you're grateful for.
2. Gratitude Jar: Decorate a jar with stickers, paint, glitter— whatever speaks to you. Each day, write what you're grateful for on a slip of paper and put it in the jar. On tough days, pull out a few slips for a quick mood boost.
3. Gratitude Prompts: Use prompts to guide your gratitude practice. For example: • I am grateful for three things I see. • I am grateful for three things I have. • I am grateful for three things in my home.

Engaging in gratitude exercises can strengthen this practice over time. Techniques such as gratitude journaling, using a gratitude jar, and employing prompts can help shift focus from negative to positive aspects of life. These exercises make gratitude a daily habit, gradually improving overall outlook and resilience.

Remember, gratitude is like a muscle— the more you use it, the stronger it gets. It might feel awkward at first, but stick with it. Before you know it, you'll be finding things to be grateful for, even in the toughest situations.

Summing It Up

As you can see, practicing gratitude does not mean that we are ignoring the bad stuff in life. Rather, it's about choosing where to focus your energy. Even in the darkest moments, there's usually a glimmer of light if you look for it.

As we move into our next chapter, keep this gratitude practice in your back pocket. It's a powerful tool that can help you navigate life's ups and downs with more grace and resilience. So, what are you grateful for today?

To fully harness the benefits of gratitude, setting SMART (Specific, Measurable, Achievable, Relevant, Time-bound) goals will help integrate gratitude practices into daily routines and ensure their effectiveness.

Reflection Questions

1. What specific aspects of gratitude do you find most challenging to incorporate into your daily life?
2. How can you apply the principles of gratitude to enhance your relationships with others?
3. What are some practical steps you can take to incorporate gratitude practices into your routine?
4. Reflect on a recent challenge you faced. How could a gratitude practice have altered your perspective or response?
5. Consider your overall health and well-being. In what ways could focusing on gratitude contribute to your physical health?

6

SMART Goals

∞

A long time ago, I was just a fresh-faced 18-year-old, three days past my birthday, signing up for the military despite my Mom's reservations. My first duty station was Fort Moore (referred to as Fort Benning at the time) in Georgia.

Now, I was an ammunition specialist. In plain language for those not in the military, I worked with explosives. And let me tell you, being the only woman in my squad was an eye-opener.

My squad leader, bless his heart, wasn't exactly a shining example of leadership. He had this habit of delegating everything to other specialists instead of leading himself. That's when it hit me— I wanted to be a better leader than that.

So right then and there, as a private, I set myself a goal. I wanted to become a sergeant, a non-commissioned officer, within three years. That was my end game, and I worked backwards from there.

I had to figure out all the requirements— computer courses, physical fitness tests, and promotion boards where they grill you on military drills and ceremonies. I laid out each step I needed to take, and you know what? I did it. Three years later, I was a non-commissioned officer.

Now, y'all might be wondering, "Monique, that's great, but what does this have to do with SMART goals?" Well, let me tell you, even though I didn't know it at the time, I was using the SMART goal framework to achieve my dream. Let's break it down and see how you can use this powerful tool in your own life.

In this chapter, we'll explore SMART goals, each letter standing for a different value. We'll also examine the benefits of using this framework and how it can transform your life, just like it did mine.

Then, I'm going to give you some practical exercises to help you set your own SMART goals. We'll focus on boosting your self-esteem and confidence because, let me tell you, there's nothing like achieving a goal to make you feel like you can take on the world.

Finally, we'll wrap up with some reflection questions to help you apply what you've learned to your own life. By the end of this chapter, you'll have the tools you need to set and achieve goals that will take you places you never thought possible.

The SMART Way

These goals are a proven and strategic approach to achieving your dreams. SMART is an acronym that stands for Specific, Measurable, Achievable, Relevant, and Time-bound. It's a framework that turns vague wishes into concrete plans.

Experts in psychology and management have long recognized the importance of goal-setting in achieving success. According to research by Ryan R. Bailey, PhD, goal-setting alone is not enough for behavior change. Instead, goals need to be well-defined and actionable (Bailey 2019). This is where the SMART criteria come into play. SMART goals provide a roadmap that clarifies what needs to be done, how success will be measured, and when it should be achieved.

Type	Definition	Example
Specific	Your goal should be clear and specific.	Instead of saying, "I want to be healthier," a specific goal would be "I will exercise for 30 minutes every day."
Measurable	Ensure that you can track your progress. A measurable goal allows you to see how far you've come.	"I will increase my exercise from 20 to 30 minutes each day" is measurable.
Achievable	Set a realistic goal that is challenging yet attainable.	If you've never exercised regularly, starting with 30 minutes a day might be more feasible than an hour.
Relevant	Your goal should align with your broader objectives and values.	If improving health is a priority, then daily exercise is a relevant goal.
Time-bound	Establish a deadline to create urgency and focus.	"I will reach my exercise goal within the next 30 days" provides a clear timeframe.

Now that we've explored the SMART framework, it's time to understand why SMART goals are effective and can enhance your commitment and enthusiasm for setting and achieving them. By examining the underlying reasons SMART goals work so well, you'll see how they can bring about real change in your life and why they are so powerful.

Why SMART Goals Work

Setting SMART goals isn't merely a matter of ticking boxes—it's about transforming your life. These goals are powerful for several reasons. First, they provide clarity by defining exactly what you're aiming for, which eliminates ambiguity and helps you stay focused. Second, SMART goals keep you motivated because you can visibly track your progress, celebrating small victories along the way. This ongoing sense of achievement fuels your drive to continue working towards your larger objective. Third, they help you prioritize by highlighting what is truly important, ensuring your efforts are directed where they will have the greatest impact. Finally, SMART goals increase your confidence; as you accomplish smaller, manageable tasks, you build self-belief and reinforce your ability to achieve bigger aspirations.

Putting SMART goals into practice involves creating actionable steps that align with each component. These exercises are designed to help you build confidence and track your progress effectively. Let's explore practical examples to get you started.

Your Turn to Set SMART Goals

Having understood the principles of SMART goals, it's time to put theory into practice. In this section, we'll explore some practical exercises designed to help you implement the SMART framework effectively. These exercises are crafted to boost your self-esteem, enhance your confidence, and turn your aspirations into achievable milestones.

	Example Ways to Get SMART
Daily Affirmation Practice	• Specific: Practice saying positive affirmations 3 times a day. • Measurable: Use a journal to record your affirmations daily. • Achievable: Start with three affirmations—that's manageable. • Relevant: Choose affirmations that address your self-esteem challenges. • Time-bound: Commit to this practice for 30 days.
Physical Activity Practice	• Specific: Engage in an activity you enjoy for 30 minutes, 3 times a week. • Measurable: Track your workouts in an app or journal. • Achievable: Start at a manageable intensity and increase gradually. • Relevant: Choose an exercise you actually like doing. • Time-bound: Maintain this routine for at least 6 weeks.

Remember, physical activity isn't just good for your body—it's also a powerful mood-booster. When you exercise, your brain releases endorphins, which are chemicals that promote a sense of well-being and happiness. This natural uplift can clear your mind of stress and anxiety, making it easier to focus on and tackle other goals in your life. Regular physical activity also increases your energy levels, enhancing your overall motivation and productivity. Whether it's a brisk walk, a dance class, or a workout at the gym, integrating physical activity into your routine can create a positive ripple effect in all areas of your life.

Now, it's time to apply these insights to your own goals. To start, ask yourself these questions:

1. What's one area of your life where you'd like to see improvement? Take a moment to reflect on aspects of your life that could benefit from change. It could be anything from your career, personal relationships, or health and wellness.

2. How can you turn that desire into a SMART goal? Break down your desire into a SMART goal by making it Specific, Measurable, Achievable, Relevant, and Time-bound. This will help you create a clear, actionable plan.

3. What potential obstacles might you face, and how can you plan for them? Consider the challenges you might encounter along the way and strategize how you will overcome them. This could include identifying resources, seeking support, or developing contingency plans.

4. Who can you share your goal with for accountability? Find someone who can support and hold you accountable. This could be a friend, mentor, or coach who can provide encouragement and check in on your progress.

5. How will achieving this goal align with your values and long-term vision for your life? Ensure that your goal reflects your core values

and contributes to your broader life vision. This alignment will make your efforts more meaningful and motivating.

By engaging in these activities, you'll gain hands-on experience setting and achieving SMART goals. You'll witness firsthand how these structured goals can lead to meaningful progress, transforming your aspirations into reality. Taking the time to work through these steps will not only enhance your goal-setting skills but also pave the way for personal growth and success.

Summing It Up

By setting Specific, Measurable, Achievable, Relevant, and Time-bound goals, you lay a solid foundation for achieving your dreams. This structured approach ensures that you stay focused, measure your progress, and adjust your strategies as needed. The benefits of SMART goals extend beyond mere task completion; they build confidence, align with your values, and contribute to your long-term vision.

As you prepare to set your own SMART goals, remember that the journey is as important as the destination. Engage with the process, stay adaptable, and celebrate each milestone along the way. This methodical approach not only helps you achieve your objectives but also fosters personal growth and a sense of fulfillment.

With this understanding of SMART goals, you're now ready to put these principles into practice.

Reflection Questions

1. What is one area of your life where you'd like to see improvement?
2. How can you turn that desire into a SMART goal?
3. What potential obstacles might you face, and how can you plan for them?
4. Who can you share your goal with for accountability?
5. How will achieving this goal align with your values and long-term vision for your life?

7

Moving on "Elevate"

∞

Although I didn't realize it then, my experiences in 2019 and during the COVID-19 pandemic marked the start of my journey into mindset coaching.

I had just returned to the States after living in Milan, Italy, for three years. I landed in Philadelphia for a new job, and with no friends or family around, I found myself living in Airbnbs, looking for a home to buy.

Then, four months later… *boom*! The pandemic struck, and I ended up Airbnb-hopping for eight whole months.

Now, let me tell you, this was no picnic. My first Airbnb? It was a windowless basement that made me feel like a prisoner. The second one? Brand new host, cleanliness issues, backed-up toilets, you name it. Finally, I landed in my third Airbnb, where I spent six months.

Even so, I ended up living in this one room, working and living for 20 hours a day. The fear of going outside was real. But you know what? Being alone for that long gives you plenty of time to think and reflect.

That's when it hit me… *I wasn't fulfilled.*

I wasn't happy just working a job that didn't bring me joy. So I asked myself, "What would bring me joy?" The answer was clear as day: traveling.

This realization prompted me to share the lessons I'd gained from over 20 years of living and working overseas with other women. My experiences encompassed the confidence I'd built, the fears I'd conquered, finding my voice, and learning to navigate different cultures.

So, right there, in the middle of a pandemic, I started my business and my charity organization. Looking back now, I realize this was the foundation for this book. It was about shifting my mindset, recognizing the gap in my life, and making a plan to fill it.

Key Concepts: The Pillars of "Elevate"

Now, let's recap what we've learned in this "Elevate" section:

1. Self-awareness: We talked about recognizing our thought patterns and understanding how they shape our reality.
2. Thinking Traps: We learned to identify and avoid common mental pitfalls that hold us back.
3. Positive Affirmations: We discovered the power of speaking positivity into our lives.
4. Gratitude: We explored how focusing on what we're thankful for can shift our entire perspective.
5. SMART Goals: We learned how to set goals that are Specific, Measurable, Achievable, Relevant, and Time-bound.

Actionable Steps

So, what can you do to start elevating your life right now? Here are some actionable steps:

Putting "Elevate" Into Practice	
Start a Daily Gratitude Practice	Every day, take a few moments to write down three things you're grateful for. This simple habit can shift your focus from what you lack to the abundance already present in your life, fostering a positive outlook and increased resilience.
Create and Repeat Positive Affirmations	Develop a set of positive affirmations tailored to your personal goals and needs. Repeat these affirmations daily, preferably in front of a mirror, to reinforce self-belief and counteract negative self-talk.
Set a SMART Goal for the Next Month	Choose one specific, measurable, achievable, relevant, and time-bound goal to focus on for the next month. Break this goal down into smaller, manageable weekly actions.
Practice Self-Awareness through Journaling	Dedicate time each day to journal about your thoughts and emotions. This practice can help you understand your internal landscape, recognize patterns, and gain insights into your behavior and motivations. Use prompts like "What am I feeling right now?" or "What events today impacted my mood?"

Challenge Negative Thought Patterns	Identify one negative thought pattern that frequently arises and challenge it using techniques discussed earlier. For example, if you often think, "I can't do this," counter it with evidence of past successes or reframe it positively: "This is challenging, but I can learn and improve." Document your progress and reflect on how changing your thought patterns affects your overall mindset.

By implementing these actionable steps, you'll be actively working towards elevating your life. Each of these practices builds upon the others, creating a holistic approach to personal growth and empowerment. Whether it's through gratitude, affirmations, goal-setting, self-awareness, or challenging negativity, you'll gain valuable tools to enhance your well-being and achieve your aspirations.

Expanding Your Horizons: What's Next?

As we wrap up "Elevate," I want you to remember something Ginni Rometty once said: "Growth and comfort do not coexist." That's what our next section, "Expand," is all about.

In "Expand," we're going to push beyond our comfort zones. We'll explore how a growth mindset can help you reach your full potential instead of being held back by limiting beliefs. We'll talk about embracing new experiences, overcoming fears, and surrounding yourself with people who lift you up.

Remember, elevation is just the first step. Now, it's time to expand those horizons and see just how far you can go.

SESSION 2: EXPAND

8

From Elevation to Expansion

"Growth and comfort do not coexist." - **Ginni Rometty**

∞

A significant shift in my thinking came when I started my journey with SWOLE (Soaring W/O Limits Enterprises), my travel agency business. I had to shed long-held limiting self-beliefs I had of myself and embrace a growth mindset. We will go into more detail about SWOLE in the next chapter. What you need to know for now is that at the start, my mind was buzzing with doubts.

Where am I going to find the time to run a business and work full-time?

What makes me qualified?

Will women even want to do business with me?

Do I have what it takes to be a successful entrepreneur?

These thoughts were like a broken record, playing over and over. But, I realized these doubts were just fear in disguise. I was stepping into new territory, and that's scary! But then I reminded myself, "Monique, you've been here before. Every time you've faced a new challenge, you've found a way to flourish. This is no different."

Self-reflection played a crucial role in overcoming my initial doubts. I had to consciously remind myself of past challenges I'd conquered and skills I'd developed. This practice of recalling previous successes became a powerful tool in building my confidence. It's a strategy I encourage you to adopt: when faced with self-doubt, take a moment to reflect on your past achievements. You'll often find that you're more capable than you give yourself credit for.

Reframing those negative thoughts into positive ones wasn't just crucial for my success. It was key to adopting a growth mindset. And once I overcame that first hurdle, my confidence soared. I was ready to wade deeper into those uncharted waters of entrepreneurship.

Fast forward three years, and not only did I start the SWOLE travel agency, but I also became a public speaker, founded an online community for women in male-dominated fields, authored three books, and started a podcast.

Can you believe it? Just imagine what you could accomplish if you expand your mindset to a growth posture!

Now, let's talk about what "expand" really means. It's about stretching beyond what you think you're capable of and challenging those long-held beliefs that have been holding you back.

First, we'll tackle those limiting beliefs head-on. You know, those little voices that say "you can't" or "you're not good enough." We'll identify them, challenge them, and replace them with empowering thoughts that propel you forward.

Next, we'll discuss embracing new experiences. Life's too short to stay in your comfort zone. We'll cover strategies for seeking out new challenges and opportunities, even when they scare you.

Speaking of comfort zones, we'll learn how to step out of them. It might feel uncomfortable at first, but that's where growth happens. Remember, growth and comfort don't coexist!

We'll also reframe how we think about failure. Instead of fearing it, we'll see it as a stepping stone to success. Every "failure" is a lesson in disguise, and we'll learn how to embrace them.

Lastly, we'll focus on surrounding ourselves with supportive and uplifting individuals who encourage personal growth. You've heard the saying, " You're the average of the five people you spend the most time with," right? We'll make sure those five people are pushing you to be your best self.

In my journey, I discovered the immense value of seeking guidance from those who've walked similar paths. When I started SWOLE, I worked with a business coach who helped me navigate the unfamiliar terrain of entrepreneurship. We will explain this in detail shortly. For now, keep in mind that while their advice was invaluable, I also learned the importance of trusting my own instincts and vision. Remember, mentors and coaches can provide direction, but ultimately, you steer your ship. Don't be afraid to seek help, but also trust in your own abilities and intuition.

Here's the lesson I want you to take away: Those beliefs you've been carrying around about yourself? They might not be your truth anymore. You're capable of so much more than you think.

By embracing a growth mindset, you're setting yourself up for success in your self-improvement journey. You're opening doors you didn't even know existed.

FROM ELEVATION TO EXPANSION

It's important to understand that expansion is not a one-time event but an ongoing process. Even now, years into my entrepreneurial journey, I still encounter new challenges that push me to grow. The key is to embrace this continuous evolution. Each new experience, whether it's writing a book, starting a podcast, or venturing into public speaking, brings its own set of challenges and opportunities for growth. Embrace them all with an open mind and a willingness to learn.

Why am I teaching you this? Because I want you to reach your highest potential. I don't want you holding yourself back because of some negative mindset. You've got greatness inside you, and it's time to let it shine!

9

Limited Self-Beliefs and Self-Imposed Limitations

"The only thing standing between you and your goal is the story you keep telling yourself as to why you can't achieve it." - **Jordan Belfort**

∞

It was 2020, and the world had come to a standstill due to the pandemic. Like many others around the country, I found myself with an abundance of time, sitting at home, contemplating my life. A realization hit me…

I am not satisfied with my life as it stands —just working, I thought to myself. *I want to do something that lights my soul up.*

For me, that something was traveling. I had always been the unofficial trip planner among my friends, coordinating adventures across the globe. So, I asked myself, "What if I could turn this passion into a business?" And so, the idea of SWOLE was born, a venture to help other women experience the joys of travel. We mentioned this before, and now I'm thrilled to reveal more about the biggest undertaking of my life.

LIMITED SELF-BELIEFS AND SELF-IMPOSED LIMITATIONS

However, as successful as SWOLE is now, my doubts set in almost immediately after I had the idea.

I'm working full-time, I worried. *How am I going to manage a full-time job and start a business?* The thought of expanding my capabilities was daunting, but I knew I had to try.

As I mentioned earlier, I sought the help of a business coach during the early days of my entrepreneurial journey. She laid out all the steps needed to set up the foundation of the business, which overwhelmed me. I had a thought that is very common for business owners who are just starting out: *How am I going to find the time for this?*

It was during that crazy first year when something surprising happened: A friend came to me with a particularly unusual message.

"Monique," she said, her eyes bright, "I had a dream about you. I saw you on stage, speaking and helping countless women.

I laughed it off. "Yeah, alright," I replied, dismissing the idea.

Public speaking had never been on my radar. I didn't like being the center of attention and always thought I wasn't a good speaker. So, whenever I thought about my friend's dream, I told myself, *that can't be me*!

I was unable to see that potential within, but life has a funny way of pushing us towards our destiny.

In 2022, another coach approached me during a call. "Monique, have you ever thought about doing public speaking?" she asked.

I burst out laughing, remembering my friend's dream from the year before. "That's so funny," I said, "My friend told me the same thing last year."

Again, I dismissed the idea, not seeing the value in what I had to say. I didn't believe I could articulate myself effectively. *How could I possibly inspire others when I couldn't even face an audience without anxiety?*

The coach persisted, "I truly believe you would be good at it. You have a good story."

It was at that moment that something shifted within me. If multiple people were seeing this potential, maybe there was some truth to it. Maybe I did have something valuable to say.

So, I *expanded* my mindset. I took a leap into the unknown, embraced my fears, and accomplished much more than I ever could have imagined.

Defining Limited Self-Beliefs and Self-Imposed Limitations

Before we can overcome these obstacles, it's crucial to understand what they are and how they differ.

Limited self-beliefs are internal beliefs that constrain what you think you can achieve. They often stem from past experiences, societal expectations, or negative self-talk. These beliefs are typically subconscious and can be deeply ingrained, making them harder to recognize and change. For example, believing you're not good at math can deter you from pursuing careers that require mathematical skills, even if you have the potential to excel in those fields.

Self- imposed limitations, on the other hand, are conscious or unconscious restrictions you place on yourself, often as a result of limited self-beliefs. They manifest as actions or decisions that prevent you from reaching your highest potential. For instance, you might not apply for a promotion because you believe you're not qualified, even if you meet all the requirements. Unlike limited self-beliefs, self-imposed limitations are actions or behaviors that result from one's beliefs.

Scenario	Limited Self-Beliefs Example	Self-Imposed Limitations Example
Career	Believing you're not capable of leading a team due to past failures in group projects.	Choosing not to apply for a leadership position because you doubt your ability to manage effectively.
Relationships	Believing you're not worthy of a healthy relationship due to past experiences or negative self-talk.	Avoiding dating or not committing to a meaningful relationship because you feel unworthy or incapable of being a good partner.
Health	Thinking you can't achieve fitness goals because you've struggled with weight issues in the past.	Avoiding exercise programs or healthy eating habits because you believe you'll never be able to stick with them.

Understanding the difference is crucial because it helps us identify the root cause of our limitations and address them effectively. Now that we've clarified the distinctions between these limitations, it's also important to understand the underlying theories that explain why these mental barriers have such a powerful impact.

Uncovering My Roots of Limitation

As I reflected on my journey, from doubting my ability to run a business to considering public speaking, I realized how much I had already expanded. Starting SWOLE had been just the beginning. In the span of three years, I had become a business owner, founded an online community called the Triple E Tribe, authored a book, and even started a podcast.

Looking back, I marveled at how far I'd come.

We are *capable* of expanding, *capable* of so much more, but we have to be *open* to trying new things in order to see how much we are capable of and where that expansion can come into play.

It wasn't until 2023 that I finally sat back and decided to pinpoint the root of these limiting self-beliefs regarding public speaking. As I reflected, I traced it back to a specific moment in my childhood— having to take speech classes in 3rd grade because I couldn't pronounce certain words. This early experience had planted a seed of inadequacy that had grown over the years, shaping my beliefs about my speaking abilities.

But it wasn't just about pronunciation. I realized this belief was also a result of deeper trauma. Over the years, I had unconsciously formed a coping mechanism to help me deal with speaking in public. I would blink my eyes repeatedly and keep blinking to the point that some people thought I was napping. If I didn't have to look at you, this allowed me to communicate without pressure. All my life, the idea of standing on a stage, all eyes on me, seemed like an impossible feat.

Despite these deeply ingrained fears and doubts, I made a pivotal decision. I decided that my message needed to be heard. It was bigger than my limiting beliefs. By coming out and sharing my story, I would enable countless women to face their fears and overcome their own limited self-beliefs. I could serve as an example for others to follow.

This personal journey of overcoming my fears and limiting beliefs about public speaking is just one example of how our own thoughts can hold us back from reaching our full potential.

The Theory Behind Limited Self-Beliefs and Self-Imposed Limitations

The concept of limited self-beliefs and self-imposed limitations is rooted in cognitive psychology and self-efficacy theory. Albert Bandura, a renowned psychologist, introduced the concept of self-efficacy, which refers to an individual's belief in their ability to succeed in specific situations or accomplish a task (Cherry, 2024).

According to Bandura's theory, people with high self-efficacy, that is, those who believe they can perform well, are more likely to view difficult tasks as something to be mastered rather than something to be avoided. On the other hand, those with low self-efficacy are more likely to avoid challenging tasks and believe that difficult goals are beyond their capabilities.

This theory explains why limited self-beliefs can be so detrimental. When we believe we're not capable of something, we're less likely to try and, therefore, less likely to succeed. This creates a self-fulfilling prophecy that reinforces our initial belief.

Carol Dweck's research on growth mindset vs. fixed mindset also contributes to our understanding of these concepts. Now, we have mentioned the "growth mindset" a few times before, but it's also important to think of it in terms of its counterpart: the "fixed" mindset. Those with a fixed mindset believe their abilities are static and unchangeable, leading to self-imposed limitations. In contrast, those with a growth mindset believe they can develop their abilities through effort and learning, which helps them overcome limiting beliefs.

Practices to Battle Limited Self-Beliefs and Self-Imposed Limitations

Here are some practical strategies that can help us battle these limiting beliefs and unlock our full potential.

Identify Your Limiting Beliefs: The first step in overcoming limited self-beliefs is to identify them. Take time to introspect and uncover the negative thoughts that may be holding you back. This process often requires deep self-reflection and honesty.

Start by setting aside quiet time for journaling. Ask yourself probing questions. *What stories do you tell yourself about your abilities? What do you believe you can't do?*

Challenge Your Beliefs: Once you've identified your limiting beliefs, it's time to challenge them. This step involves critically examining the validity of these beliefs and questioning their origins.

For each limiting belief you've identified, ask yourself: *Are these beliefs valid? Are they based on facts or assumptions?*

Often, we'll find that our limiting beliefs are not grounded in reality but in unfounded fears about the future or past experiences that are no longer relevant. By challenging these beliefs, you begin to loosen their hold on you.

Reframe Negative Thoughts: Transform each limiting belief into a positive, empowering statement. For example, change "I'm not good at public speaking" to "I can improve my public speaking skills with practice." Or, reframe "I'm too old to start a new career" to "My experience gives me a unique advantage in my new field." Shift negative self-talk to growth-focused affirmations that encourage progress and confidence.

Practice Visualization

Visualization is a powerful tool used by athletes, entrepreneurs, and performers to overcome self-doubt and achieve their goals.

Set aside time daily to picture yourself succeeding:

1. Find a quiet, comfortable space.
2. Close your eyes, breathe deeply, and relax.
3. Imagine yourself overcoming your limiting beliefs, fully engaging all your senses.
4. Focus on how success looks and feels.

By regularly practicing visualization, you can rewire your brain to make success feel more attainable and natural .

Celebrate Small Wins: Any step towards changing your negative thought patterns is a win. Celebrate that you took action, no matter how small. This positive reinforcement can help build momentum and confidence.

Seek Professional Help: If limiting beliefs stem from past traumas or deep psychological patterns, consider seeking help from a therapist. They can offer tools and strategies to overcome these beliefs.

By applying these practices consistently, you can break free from limiting beliefs and self-imposed limitations, becoming more confident, resilient, and open to new opportunities.

10

How Not to Fear Failure

"Success is not final, failure is not fatal: it is the courage to continue that counts." - **Winston Churchill**

∞

The fear of failure is a universal experience, but it doesn't have to control our lives or limit our potential. Let me share a personal story that illustrates how facing the possibility of failure can lead to unexpected growth and self-discovery.

I can remember, as early as 14 years old, desiring to have twins, a boy and a girl. I had a name book, and I would jot down the corresponding names for him and her. I knew without a shadow of a doubt that motherhood would be a part of my future. As it turned out, my career became the forefront of my life, and I put motherhood on the back burner. I thought that I had time, but before I knew it, I felt as if my biological clock was a time bomb that was due to explode at any moment.

At 45 years old, I decided to make my desire for motherhood a reality and embarked upon the journey of artificial insemination to help me create the family I longed for. At every turn, I was told that my chances of success were minimal. My doctor advised me that due to my age, my eggs were not viable. Friends and family believed I was too old to be a mother. Even though the cards were stacked against me, I still proceeded forward anyway because, to me, not even trying was unfathomable.

Technically, since the end result did not result in a pregnancy, this would be considered a failure by definition. However, I share this story with you to illustrate that we shouldn't let the fear of failure or naysayers stop us from pursuing the desires of our hearts. You never know what blessings are waiting for you on the other side of your "yes."

Defining Failure

Before we can overcome the fear of failure, it's important to understand what failure really is. Failure is often defined as a lack of success or the inability to meet an expectation. However, many experts argue that this definition is too narrow and doesn't capture the full complexity of failure in the context of personal growth and achievement.

Carol Dweck, a renowned psychologist and author of *Mindset: The New Psychology of Success*, argues that our perception of failure is closely tied to our mindset. Those with a fixed mindset tend to view failure as a reflection of their inherent abilities and worth (Dweck, 2006). In contrast, those with a growth mindset see failure as an opportunity for learning and improvement.

Another perspective comes from Sara Blakely, the founder of Spanx, who credits her success to her father's unique approach to failure. He would ask her and her brother what they had failed at each week, celebrating their attempts rather than their successes (Hunter, 2018). This reframing of failure as a positive sign of effort and learning can significantly reduce the fear associated with it.

Understanding the nature of failure is the first step toward effectively managing it. Once we recognize that failure is an inevitable part of growth, it's crucial to adopt strategies that help us navigate it constructively.

Practices to Battle Fear of Failure

Here are some practical approaches to overcoming the fear of failure and transforming setbacks into opportunities for improvement.

Tip	Explanation
Acceptance of Failure	Use failure as a learning tool. After a failed project, analyze what went wrong to improve future efforts.
Show Yourself Grace	Reframe failure as a growth opportunity, not self-condemnation. If a presentation doesn't go well, focus on lessons learned.
Get Out of Your Head	Avoid over-analyzing by seeking feedback from a trusted mentor to gain perspective.
Do It Afraid	Push through fear by taking action. Apply for a promotion even if you're unsure, recognizing that growth comes from discomfort.

This summarizes the practical approaches to managing failure and provides concrete examples to illustrate each strategy.

My Journey Continues

As for me, my journey of overcoming my fear of public speaking didn't end with that realization in 2023. It was just the beginning. I decided to face my fear head-on and started small, speaking at local events and workshops. Each time I spoke, my confidence grew a little more.

Yes, there were moments of nervousness and self-doubt. There were times when I stumbled over my words or lost my train of thought. But I reminded myself that perfection wasn't the goal —progress was. I celebrated each small victory, each time I pushed through my fear and spoke anyway.

I also sought out support. I joined a local Toastmasters group, where I could practice speaking in a supportive environment. I worked with a coach who helped me develop my speaking skills and manage my anxiety. And I surrounded myself with friends and colleagues who believed in me, even when I struggled to believe in myself.

Gradually, my extended blinks became less frequent. I found myself making eye contact more easily. And most importantly, I started to see the value in my message and my ability to deliver it.

Today, while I can't say I'm entirely free of nerves when I speak in public, I can say that I no longer let those nerves hold me back. I've spoken at conferences and led many workshops. Each of these experiences has reinforced what I now know to be true: our limiting beliefs don't define us unless we let them.

My story of overcoming my fear of public speaking is just one example of how we can push past our limiting beliefs and self-imposed limitations. Your story might be different. Perhaps you've always believed you're not creative, that you're not leadership material, or that you're too old to start a new career. Whatever your limiting belief is, I want you to know that it's possible to overcome it.

Summing It Up

It won't always be easy. There will be setbacks and moments of doubt. But with persistence, self-compassion, and the right support, you can rewrite the stories you tell yourself. You can expand your sense of what's possible and step into a fuller, more authentic version of yourself.

As we move into the next chapter, I encourage you to carry this message with you: You are capable of so much more than you think. Your limiting beliefs are just that— beliefs, not facts. And beliefs can be changed. So dream bigger, reach higher, and don't let your own thoughts be the thing that holds you back from achieving your full potential.

The journey of a thousand miles begins with a single step. What step will you take today to challenge your limiting beliefs and expand your horizons? The power to change your life lies within you.

Reflection Questions

1. What beliefs have you held since childhood?
2. What are you really afraid of?
3. What thoughts arise when you face new challenges?
4. How do you respond to moments of self-doubt?
5. Recall a time you proved your limiting beliefs wrong.
6. Does your inner circle challenge your limiting beliefs or reinforce them?
7. What small step can you take to challenge your limiting beliefs?
8. What if you succeed?

11

Embrace New Experiences, Challenges, and Step Out of Your Comfort Zone

"Life begins at the end of your comfort zone." - **Neale Donald Walsch**

∞

In 2016, I found myself at a crossroads. I was working for the federal government in Maryland, but I was looking for a change. That's when an opportunity crossed my path that seemed too good to pass up.... a chance to live and work in Milan, Italy, for three years.

Italy? Europe? I thought to myself. All I could think about was Europe and all the exciting experiences that awaited me. Images of romantic canals, exquisite cuisine, and rich history flooded my mind.

Without hesitation, I accepted the opportunity.

Little did I know that accepting this job would thrust me into a whirlwind of challenges and feelings of self-doubt that would push me far beyond my comfort zone.

On my first day in the office, the reality of my new position hit me like a ton of bricks.

"Welcome," my new colleague said. "You'll be the lead of this new operation. We're starting pretty much from ground zero."

My jaw dropped. "Lead? New operation?" I stammered.

He nodded, continuing, "You'll have cognizance over eight countries and be traveling 50% of each month—countries like Bosnia, Bulgaria, Serbia…"

As he spoke, a wave of fear washed over me.

"Oh, and there's no established team or procedures yet," he added casually.

I felt my stomach churn.

How was I going to manage this?

I must admit that my initial reaction was one of fear and self-doubt. None of these details had been disclosed to me during the interview process. On top of all this, I would be venturing to these countries *alone*, many of which I had never visited before. I had concerns about my safety, language barriers, and the fact that I wouldn't see anyone who looked like me for extended periods.

This position presented a new challenge on multiple fronts. I hadn't been in a supervisory role for over ten years, and I'd never held a position with such vast requirements. I was well outside of my comfort zone, to say the least. To not only survive in this role but to thrive, I knew I had to shift my mindset. I needed to embrace this challenge as an opportunity for growth and see it as a stepping stone to bigger and greater things.

EMBRACE NEW EXPERIENCES, CHALLENGES, AND STEP OUT OF YOUR COMFORT ZONE

Reflecting on my previous experiences helped me find the internal fortitude to recognize that I was qualified for this position. I reminded myself that I was hired because someone believed in my capabilities. This self-reflection became a crucial tool in boosting my confidence and tackling the challenges ahead.

As I faced each new obstacle, whether it was navigating a foreign city, communicating with non-English speakers, or making critical decisions without immediate support, I found myself growing both personally and professionally. Each small victory built my resilience and expanded my comfort zone.

In the end, my team's hard work and perseverance paid off. We ended up winning team of the quarter, and I was honored with the Employee of the Quarter award. Looking back, I can't help but wonder, "What if I hadn't accepted this challenge?" I would have never known I was capable of so much more.

So, to you, the reader, I say this: when faced with a daunting challenge, remember to pull from your past highlights. Reflect on what you've accomplished before, whether professionally or personally. Let those memories empower you to take on new experiences and challenges because it's by stepping out of our comfort zones that we truly unleash our full potential. It's now time to take a look at why this is so important and how you can apply this principle in your own life.

How Embracing New Challenges Helps You Grow Personally and Professionally

By this point, you understand that we , as humans, often encounter situations that push us beyond our comfort zones. These challenges, while sometimes daunting, are actually golden opportunities for growth and self-discovery. When we embrace these challenges rather than shying away from them, we open ourselves up to a world of personal and professional development. These are the numerous ways in which facing challenges head-on can benefit us:

1. **Builds Resilience:** Each challenge you face and overcome builds your confidence and empowers you to face new challenges. The more you push yourself, the more resilient you become. This self-assurance carries over into future challenges, making you more likely to approach them with a "can-do" attitude rather than fear or hesitation.

2. **Expands Your Comfort Zone:** Being willing to step outside your comfort zone reveals new strengths and capabilities you may not have otherwise been aware of. As you tackle new experiences, what once seemed impossible becomes achievable. This growth is invaluable in both personal and professional settings, allowing you to take on greater responsibilities and challenges with confidence.

3. **Enhances Learning and Adaptation:** Challenges often leave us with valuable lessons. If you're willing to embrace the challenge, you'll find that it's a critical aspect of personal development. Each new situation teaches you something about yourself and the world around you. By approaching challenges with a learning mindset, you transform potentially stressful situations into opportunities for growth and self-improvement.

4. **Sharpens Problem-Solving Skills:** Addressing challenges hones your problem-solving capabilities. This is an invaluable skill in any professional environment. The more diverse challenges you face, the more creative and adaptable your problem-solving skills become. These

skills are transferable across various aspects of your life, making you more effective in your career and personal endeavors.

5. **Boosts Creativity:** Facing challenges often forces you to think outside the box. This supports innovation, another useful tool in professional environments. When you're pushed out of your comfort zone, you're more likely to come up with novel solutions and ideas. By regularly challenging yourself, you train your mind to be more flexible and imaginative in its thinking.

Embracing challenges and new experiences is a powerful way to unlock your potential and grow both personally and professionally. However, knowing the benefits of stepping out of your comfort zone is only half the battle. The next crucial step is learning how to effectively embrace these new experiences and navigate the challenges they bring.

From Panic to Possibility

One of my biggest fears for as long as I can remember was getting lost and not being able to find my way. This fear came to life during a work trip to Belgrade, Serbia. While driving on the highway, my TomTom device suddenly died, and I found myself in a panic. Serbia is not a predominantly English-speaking country, and the thought of navigating through unfamiliar streets without assistance felt overwhelming. How was I going to find my hotel?

I took a few deep breaths to calm myself down. When I looked up, I saw a highway sign with "Belgrade" written in English. I figured that if I followed the signs, I'd at least get closer to where I needed to be. I arrived in the city and stopped at a small boutique where I met a young woman who spoke English. Relieved, I asked her to call me a cab and gave her the address of my hotel. I decided to follow the cab driver in my car, trusting that this would guide me safely to my destination.

That experience became a turning point for me. I had faced one of my worst fears and overcame it , unlocking a new sense of confidence. Not only did I find my way, but the whole ordeal taught me that I was far more capable than I had ever given myself credit for. This experience was also the catalyst that opened me up to solo travel. I realized I no longer had to wait for others to explore the world—I could do it on my own.

After that trip, I embraced the challenge of seeing the world solo. During my time in Europe, I went on to visit 23 countries. Each new destination became an opportunity to step further out of my comfort zone and discover more about myself.

This story is not just about navigating a foreign country ; it's about embracing new experiences and challenges. Whether it's facing a fear or tackling something unfamiliar, these moments of discomfort often lead to our greatest growth. Now, I want to share some tips with you on how to embrace new challenges and open yourself to the world of possibilities that await you.

Tips for Embracing New Experiences

Stepping into the unknown can be exciting but also intimidating. Whether you're starting a new job, moving to a new city, or trying something outside your usual routine, here are some strategies to help you embrace new experiences with confidence and optimism.

Seek a Mentor: A mentor who has navigated similar challenges can provide valuable insights and support. For example, imagine a software developer transitioning into a leadership role. They reach out to a trusted project manager for guidance, learning practical ways to balance new responsibilities. Through these conversations, they gradually feel more prepared and confident in their ability to lead.

Reflect on Past Changes: Look back on how you've handled changes in the past five years. You might be surprised at how adaptable you've already been. Reflecting on past experiences can boost your confidence in facing new challenges. For instance, before a solo backpacking trip, recalling how you moved cities, started a new job, or navigated personal changes could make the future seem less daunting and spark excitement.

Assess What's in Your Control: List things you can and can't control in your current situation. Focus on what you can influence and let go of what's outside your control. For example, during a company merger, you might focus on improving your skills and maintaining relationships rather than worrying about restructuring decisions.

Amp Up Your Self-Care Routine: Stress often accompanies change, so make sure to prioritize self-care. Incorporate activities like meditation, exercise, or a favorite hobby to manage stress and stay balanced. For instance, a graduate student facing intense pressure might commit to daily meditation, regular gym time, and a creative hobby, helping them stay calm and focused amidst the demands of their program.

Summing It Up:

Let's return to that office in Milan, where I stood facing an unexpected and daunting challenge. What seemed like a dream opportunity quickly transformed into a test of my resilience and adaptability. Yet, it was precisely this challenge that propelled me to new heights, both personally and professionally.

My journey in Milan serves as a snapshot of the growth that awaits us when we dare to step out of our comfort zones. Like the diverse countries I had to navigate— Bosnia, Bulgaria, and Serbia— each new experience we embrace is a territory waiting to be explored. And just as I had to build a team from the ground up, you, too, must construct your own toolkit for embracing change and challenges.

Remember, your life is not a static tableau but a dynamic landscape. Each new experience, whether it's seeking a mentor, reflecting on past changes, assessing what's in your control, or amping up your self-care routine, adds a brushstroke to this ever-evolving masterpiece. These aren't just strategies; they're the vibrant colors that bring depth and richness to your personal and professional life.

As you stand at the threshold of your own "Milan ," whatever that may be for you, know that the uncertainty you feel is not a stop sign but a starting line. The challenges ahead are not obstacles but opportunities disguised as difficulties. They are invitations to discover strengths you never knew you possessed and to expand your horizons beyond what you thought possible.

But here's a crucial insight I gained from my experience: *we don't have to face these challenges alone.*

In fact, the journey becomes not just easier, but infinitely more rewarding when we surround ourselves with the right people. This brings us to our next chapter, where we'll explore the profound impact of surrounding yourself with supportive and uplifting individuals who encourage personal growth.

EMBRACE NEW EXPERIENCES, CHALLENGES,
AND STEP OUT OF YOUR COMFORT ZONE

Reflection Questions

As you consider how to embrace new experiences and challenges in your own life, take some time to reflect on these questions:

1. In what ways have you grown and changed over the last year?

2. How do you define personal growth for yourself?

3. How do you currently push yourself out of your comfort zone? Are there areas where you could challenge yourself more?

4. How do you handle failure, and what does it teach you?

5. What beliefs do you hold that may limit your personal growth?

6. What steps are you taking to create a more fulfilling life?

7. What's one new experience or challenge you've been avoiding? What's holding you back?

8. How can you reframe your thinking about this challenge to see it as an opportunity for growth?

12

Surround Yourself with Supportive and Uplifting Individuals Who Encourage Personal Growth

"If you want to go fast, go alone. If you want to go far, go together."
- African Proverb

∞

The power of surrounding yourself with the right people cannot be overstated. I learned this lesson firsthand upon returning from my transformative experience in Italy. Little did I know that the next chapter of my personal growth journey was about to unfold, all thanks to a simple introduction from a friend.

In the latter part of 2019, I was introduced to a women's group called Soul Wealth. From the moment I joined, I was struck by the caliber of women in this group. These weren't just any group of women; they were powerhouses in their own right. The majority were successful entrepreneurs, authors, and public speakers, each accomplished in her own field.

SURROUND YOURSELF WITH SUPPORTIVE AND UPLIFTING INDIVIDUALS WHO ENCOURAGE PERSONAL GROWTH

Dr. Vikki Johnson, the founder of Soul Wealth, led this remarkable group. A media mogul who had graced television screens and rubbed shoulders with celebrities, her prominence added an extra layer of awe to the group's dynamic.

I'll be honest. At first, I felt intimidated. Here I was, a government employee, surrounded by women who seemed to have achieved so much more. I questioned whether I truly belonged in their midst. The stark contrast between their entrepreneurial success and my status as "just an employee" made me feel as though I didn't measure up.

But as time passed, something remarkable happened. The environment that Dr. Johnson had created was one of inclusion, sisterhood, and empowerment, and it began to work its magic on me. Instead of feeling like an outsider, I was welcomed as another sister in the group. The fear of cattiness or competition that often plagues women's groups was nowhere to be found. Instead, I found myself in a supportive, nurturing space that challenged me to see beyond my current circumstances.

As I spent more time with these incredible women and formed deeper relationships, my perspective began to shift. I started to see more capabilities within myself than I had ever recognized before. The inspiration I drew from these women was profound. Their success wasn't intimidating anymore. It was motivating.

This shift in perspective bore fruit in 2020 when I took the leap and started SWOLE. The birth of my business was largely a result of being in the midst of these inspiring women. They had shown me what was possible and, in doing so, had awakened a desire in me to explore my own potential.

The support I received from the Soul Wealth community when I launched my business was overwhelming. These women didn't just offer words of encouragement ; they became my first customers, my mentors, and my cheerleaders. Dr. Vikki Johnson, the woman I had once been in awe of, became my first podcast guest. She took me under her wing, helping me mastermind strategies to grow my business and expand into public speaking.

My experience with Soul Wealth underscores a crucial point: the people you surround yourself with can be game-changers in your personal and professional growth. Being in the right circle – one that uplifts, encourages, and empowers you can propel you to heights you never thought possible. Conversely, surrounding yourself with individuals who doubt you or hold you back can stifle your growth and limit your potential.

How Positive People Impact Your View of Yourself and the World

The impact of positive influences extends far beyond mere encouragement. When you're surrounded by individuals who believe in you, celebrate your successes, and encourage you to pursue your goals, you begin to internalize these affirmations. This shift in perspective can lead to increased self-confidence, resilience, and a more optimistic outlook on life.

These uplifting individuals often challenge you to think bigger, act with courage, and push beyond your comfort zone. They serve as role models, showing you what's possible when you approach life with a positive mindset. Over time, their influence can help you develop a growth-oriented attitude, where challenges are seen as opportunities and setbacks are viewed as temporary obstacles to overcome.

In my case, the women of Soul Wealth helped me see possibilities I had never considered before. Their success didn't make me feel small; it expanded my vision of what I could achieve. They helped me redefine my own potential and gave me the courage to step into entrepreneurship.

How to Find Good People to Surround Yourself With

Finding supportive, uplifting people requires intentional effort. Here are key strategies to help you build a positive community:

1. Engage in growth-oriented environments: Attend workshops and seminars or join communities that value personal growth and positivity.

2. Don't be afraid to initiate: Network at events, join social groups, or volunteer for causes that resonate with you. Authentic relationships often start through shared interests.

3. Be open to new relationships: Supportive people can come from unexpected places, so stay open to diverse connections.

4. Prioritize quality over quantity: A few meaningful relationships have a greater impact than a large number of superficial ones.

Look for people who inspire you: Seek out individuals who are where you want to be, whether in their personal lives or careers. Their journey can provide valuable insights and motivation.

Join or create a mastermind group: Collaborate with like-minded individuals to share ideas, provide feedback, and hold each other accountable for achieving goals.

Remember, building a positive environment is not just about finding good influences but also removing those that hinder your progress.

How to Release Negative People

While it's crucial to surround yourself with positive influences, it's equally important to distance yourself from negative ones. Releasing negative people from your life can be challenging, especially if they are long-time friends, family members, or co-workers. However, it's essential for your well-being and growth.

1. Set boundaries: Limit interactions, establish what behavior you won't tolerate, or gradually distance yourself.
2. Communicate openly: If possible, have an honest conversation about how their behavior affects you. Some may be unaware and willing to change.
3. Focus on your growth: As you invest time in personal development and positive relationships, you may naturally distance yourself from negative influences.
4. Seek support: Lean on your positive circle or a professional for guidance if needed.

Releasing negativity opens space for more positive, supportive relationships to flourish. Prioritize your well-being, not by abruptly cutting people off, but by creating room for healthier connections.

Summing It Up

The journey of personal growth is not one you have to walk alone. By surrounding yourself with supportive, uplifting individuals who encourage your growth, you create a powerful ecosystem for success. Just as the women of Soul Wealth inspired and supported me in my entrepreneurial journey, you, too, can find your tribe of cheerleaders, mentors, and supporters.

SURROUND YOURSELF WITH SUPPORTIVE AND UPLIFTING INDIVIDUALS WHO ENCOURAGE PERSONAL GROWTH

As we move forward, remember that the company you keep can elevate your dreams, expand your horizons, and empower you to reach your full potential. Choose wisely, for in the words of Jim Rohn, "You are the average of the five people you spend the most time with." Make sure those five people are pushing you towards your best self.

In our next chapter, we'll explore how to take all these lessons— from embracing challenges to surrounding yourself with positivity— and apply them to create a life of purpose and fulfillment. Are you ready to step into your power and create the life you've always dreamed of? Let's continue this journey together.

Reflection Questions

1. Who in your life consistently uplifts and supports you? What steps can you take to strengthen these relationships?
2. Are there any relationships that you find draining or negative? What steps can you take to set boundaries or release these individuals?
3. What environments or communities can you engage with to meet more positive and supportive individuals?
4. How can you become a more positive influence on others in your life?
5. What's one step you can take this week to expand your circle of positive influences?

13

Moving on to "Explore"

"The only way to make sense out of change is to plunge into it, move with it, and join the dance." - **Alan Watts**

∞

As we wrap up our journey through the "Expand" section, I'm reminded of my own path of growth and change. Just like you, I've been pushing my boundaries and expanding my horizons in ways I never thought possible.

Remember when we talked about my move to Milan and starting a business during a pandemic? Those experiences, challenging as they were, laid the groundwork for what we've been exploring in this section. They taught me firsthand the power of embracing new experiences, challenging limiting beliefs, and surrounding myself with supportive individuals.

We've learned that growth often happens when we're uncomfortable, and that's not just okay— it's necessary. We've discovered the strength that comes from pushing past our comfort zones and the wisdom gained from reframing our perspective on failure.

MOVING ON TO "EXPLORE"

But expansion, as transformative as it is, is just one part of our journey. It's opened our minds and broadened our horizons. Now, with this newfound openness and wider perspective, we're ready for the next phase of our adventure.

Key Concepts: The Pillars of "Expand"

Before we move forward, let's recap what we've learned in the "Expand" section:

1. Overcoming Limited Self-Beliefs: We discovered how to identify and challenge the beliefs that hold us back.
2. Embracing New Experiences: We learned the value of stepping out of our comfort zones and facing new challenges.
3. Reframing Failure: We shifted our perspective on failure, seeing it as a stepping stone rather than a roadblock.
4. Building a Supportive Network: We recognized the importance of surrounding ourselves with positive, uplifting individuals.

Actionable Steps

So, what can you do to start expanding your life right now? Here are some actionable steps:

Putting "Expand" Into Practice	
Step Out of Your Comfort Zone	Weekly, try something new—whether it's a hobby, speaking up, or networking. Document what you learn.
Seek New Experiences	Visit a new place, even if nearby, and reflect on how it broadens your perspective.

Practice Resilience	When facing setbacks, reframe them as learning opportunities. Keep a journal to track your growth.
Set an Expansion Goal	Pick one area of life to expand (e.g., skills, relationships) and set a 3-month goal. Break it into weekly steps.
Celebrate Your Wins	Weekly, acknowledge one way you've grown. This keeps you motivated and reinforces positive change.

Exploring New Depths: What's Next?

You're standing at the edge of a vast, unexplored forest. Behind you lies the familiar terrain we've traversed in "Expand"— the comfort zones we've pushed, the limiting beliefs we've challenged, the new experiences we've embraced. But ahead? A dense, mysterious woodland filled with untapped potential and hidden treasures.

That's where we're headed next in our "Explore" section.

As we step into this new territory, we're not just looking around ; we're looking within. We're going to dive deep into the roots of our being, examining how our mindset intertwines with our physical actions and spiritual essence. It's like we're explorers mapping the intricate ecosystem of our inner selves.

We'll discover how a holistic approach to personal growth, encompassing mental, physical, and spiritual aspects, can lead to a truly positive mindset. We'll learn to show ourselves compassion, set meaningful goals, and cultivate daily practices that nourish our souls.

MOVING ON TO "EXPLORE"

We'll uncover how our mindset correlates with our physical activities and spiritual practices. We'll explore techniques for mindfulness, self-care, and releasing the need for external validation. We'll also learn how to celebrate our progress, no matter how small, and how to implement a consistent spiritual practice that resonates with our individual beliefs.

Remember, expansion has given us a broader perspective and pushed our boundaries. Now, it's time to explore the depths of who we are and who we can become. It's time to enter that cave, face our fears, and discover the treasures within ourselves.

SESSION 3: EXPLORE

14

From Expansion to Exploration

"I will go anywhere, as long as it is forward."-**David Livingstone**

∞

People love to romanticize road trips. They talk about freedom, discovery, beautiful vistas. My experience with road trips? Pure endurance.

In 2006, I was hired as an assistant supervisor for a government contractor in Southern California. This opportunity came at an important moment in my life, as I had recently been fired from my first government job (a story we'll get into later in the book). While back home in Upstate New York, awaiting my start date, I faced one significant hurdle: how was I going to get from New York to Southern California?

Initially, I planned to make the cross-country trip with my parents. They would drive the U-Haul with my belongings, and I would follow in my car. However, when they couldn't make the trip, it became a solo adventure. So, I packed up my 1998 Pontiac Grand Prix with as much as I could, and off I went.

Soon enough, thirty-six hours of interstate stretched between me and my new life in California. Not by choice but by necessity. Just me, a car radio that didn't work, and miles of necessity ahead.

I had n o time to admire the scenery and made n o tourist stops. This wasn't a vacation; this was survival.

Twelve hours of driving each day. Sleep. Repeat. Iowa blurred into Nebraska into Colorado into Utah. My back ached. My eyes burned.

Day one's determination crumbled into day two's exhaustion. By day three, time had lost meaning. States passed in a haze of gas stations and cheap motels.

Three and a half days later, I reached California. Empty. Drained. Done.

Every mile marked another hour of solitude, another test of will. No profound insights struck me on those endless highways, just the constant reminder that sometimes growth feels more like survival than transformation.

That's the truth about personal growth, too. Not every step forward feels inspiring. Not every challenge teaches an immediate lesson. Sometimes, you just have to push through the hard parts, trusting that movement— any movement— beats standing still.

We've spent chapters discussing expansion, pushing past comfort zones, and reaching higher. Now, let's get real about what growth actually feels like. Like that road trip, transformation often comes packaged in discomfort, wrapped in necessity, driven by circumstances beyond our control.

Your self-doubt, your fear, your hesitation, I've felt them all. In those lonely hotel rooms between states, questioning every decision ; in the pre-

FROM EXPANSION TO EXPLORATION

dawn darkness, wondering if I could face another day of driving; in the silence of a broken radio, confronting every insecurity I'd tried to outrun.

The next section focuses on exploration. Not the sanitized, Instagram-worthy version, but the messy, real-life process. We'll tackle:

- Hard truths about mind-body connection when you're stressed
- Finding spiritual ground when nothing feels certain
- Building real confidence from repeated small wins
- Trusting yourself even when the path looks nothing like you expected

Some days, you'll feel strong. On other days, you'll want to turn back. Both reactions are valid. Both are part of the process.

I drove cross-country because I had to, not because I wanted to. Maybe you're here for similar reasons. Life knocked you down. Circumstances forced change. Or you're simply tired of feeling small in your own life.

Whatever brought you here, know this: Growth isn't always pretty. It isn't always inspiring. Sometimes, it's just about keeping your hands on the wheel and your eyes on the road, trusting that every mile, even the hard ones, takes you closer to where you need to be.

Take a deep breath. Check your mirrors. The road ahead leads to the real you—confident, capable, whole. Ready to drive?

The best views often come after the hardest miles.

Take a moment to reflect on your own challenging journeys. Have you ever had to push through something difficult, not because you wanted to, but because you had to? What kept you going? What did you learn about yourself in those moments of pure endurance?

While my cross-country journey was primarily physical, it taught me something profound about the connection between mind, body, and spirit. When one is pushed to its limits, the others must compensate and support. This delicate balance would become crucial in my understanding of personal growth.

15

Showing Yourself Grace and Compassion

"Be patient with yourself. Self-growth is tender; it's holy ground. There's no greater investment." **-Stephen Covey**

∞

My first real relationship began when I joined the Army at 18. My first duty station was at Fort Benning, Georgia (now known as Fort Moore). It was there that I met Aaron at the in-processing center, and we hit it off immediately. We spent most of our free time together—watching movies, going to ball games, and simply enjoying each other's company. Being with him felt exciting and new.

This relationship also marked my first experience with sex, and looking back, I was incredibly naive when it came to preventing pregnancy. I had little knowledge about what I should have been doing to protect myself. At that point, Aaron and I had been dating for about five months, but I started to notice a shift in our dynamic.

Aaron became controlling. He didn't like me hanging out with my friends, dictated what I could and couldn't eat, and refused to let me use the bathroom on his barracks floor because it was "for males only." Shockingly, I went along with it, resorting to using mason jars to relieve myself just to avoid upsetting him.

Red flags often wave brightest in hindsight. As my relationship with Aaron darkened, so did my ability to see my own worth. One day, I noticed a painful bump on my buttocks and went to the clinic to get it checked out. The doctor informed me that it was an infected cyst, and I had to stay in the hospital to have it lanced. It was during this hospital stay that I received another life-changing piece of news: I was pregnant.

Before I share what happened next, I want to talk about a practice that would have helped me during those turbulent days: mindfulness.

Understanding Mindfulness: A Path to Self-Awareness

Looking back at my younger self, I see how much I needed mindfulness skills. Instead of being present with my feelings about Aaron's controlling behavior, I pushed them aside. Rather than noticing the red flags, I rushed forward. If I had practiced mindfulness then, I might have recognized sooner that something wasn't right.

But that's why mindfulness is so important. When you use these skills, you are not beating yourself up over the past. It's about being gentle with yourself right here, right now.

Mindfulness means being fully present in each moment and accepting what's happening without judgment. Instead of getting caught up in stress or overthinking, mindfulness teaches you to tune into your thoughts, feelings, and surroundings. When your mind races to tomorrow's worries or yesterday's regrets, mindfulness gently brings you back to now.

Reflection: How often do you pause to truly experience the present moment? What keeps you from being more mindful in your daily life?

The table below will show us some intentional ways that we can practice mindfulness and provide real-life examples to put them into context.

Ways to Practice Mindfulness	
Tip	**Example**
Focus on one task fully.	Eliminate distractions, set aside your phone, and immerse yourself in the activity.
Listen attentively.	Let others finish speaking before responding, focusing on their words to connect meaningfully.
Notice small joys.	Appreciate moments like a sunrise, a kind smile, or a comforting drink to boost gratitude.
Check in with your body.	Pause daily to take deep breaths and release tension in your shoulders, jaw, or back.
Accept emotions without judgment.	Observe feelings like frustration or joy without labeling them as good or bad.

Think of mindfulness as a skill. At its heart, it's about paying attention to what's happening inside and around you without trying to change it or react right away. You simply observe. Notice. Accept. The more you practice this way of being, the better you handle life's challenges. You'll find yourself less reactive, more in control of your emotions, and better equipped to face difficult situations. In this way, each moment in life offers a fresh chance to tune in, pay attention, and make choices from a place of awareness rather than reaction.

The true power of mindfulness shows up when life gets hard. When emotions feel overwhelming, or decisions loom large, being present helps you stay grounded. You learn to observe your thoughts without getting swept away by them. You notice your feelings without drowning in them.

This kind of presence and acceptance would become crucial in my journey ahead, especially with the life-changing news I received in that hospital room. Armed with this understanding of mindfulness, let me take you back to that clinic...

Twenty Years of Silence

At 19, six months into my Army service, I faced the hardest decision of my life. I chose to terminate the pregnancy. The weight of my reality pressed in from all sides . I wasn't ready to be a mother, I feared disappointing my family, and I couldn't imagine staying connected to Aaron forever, especially after seeing his true colors.

Aaron went with me to the clinic. I still remember lying on that table, my heart pounding so hard I thought it might break through my chest. The monitor's soft glow illuminated my fears and doubts as I wondered about the heartbeat, about whether it was a boy or a girl. A deep ache of loss settled in my chest, a heaviness that would become all too familiar in the years to come. Then, the anesthesia took over, and everything went dark. Afterward, I told no one. I just went back to work like nothing had happened, though inside, I felt hollowed out, forever changed.

I missed my follow-up appointment because I had to go to a training exercise in the Southern California desert. That's when the feelings started: guilt, regret, self-blame. They didn't just visit ; they brought their luggage, moved into my brain, and lived there for twenty years. Every time I saw a baby, tears would come. I'd calculate how old my child would be, marking phantom birthdays in my mind.

Time doesn't heal all wounds. Sometimes, it just teaches us to carry them quietly. For two decades, I carried this weight alone. No one knew. No one saw. I seemed fine on the outside, while inside, a storm raged.

One morning, staring at myself in the bathroom mirror, tears streaming down my face after seeing a baby at the grocery store, I realized something had to give. This weight wasn't just affecting me anymore ; it was determining how I lived my whole life. That's when I learned about self-compassion.

Think about a burden you've been carrying. How has it shaped your decisions and behaviors? What would it feel like to begin releasing that weight?

Practicing Self-Compassion

The weight of two decades is heavy. But even the heaviest burdens can be lightened when we learn to be gentle with ourselves. When I first heard about self-compassion, I thought it meant letting myself off the hook. I was wrong. Real self-compassion means holding yourself accountable while still treating yourself with understanding.

Far from a luxury, self-compassion is a survival skill for navigating difficult times. When you're carrying heavy burdens, being kind to yourself isn't selfish, it's necessary. Here's what I've learned about practicing self-compassion.

1. Think about how you'd comfort a close friend going through hard times. You'd listen without judgment. You'd offer understanding, patience, and maybe a shoulder to cry on. Why not offer yourself that same kindness? When those harsh thoughts come up, ask yourself, "Would I say this to someone I care about?

2. It's okay to hurt. It's okay to feel frustrated or upset. Instead of pushing these feelings away or criticizing yourself for having them, simply acknowledge them. Say it out loud: "I'm feeling pain right now, and that's okay."

3. Watch how you talk to yourself when things go wrong. If you catch that inner critic getting loud, pause. Instead of "I'm such a failure," try "I made the best decision I could with what I knew at the time."

Moving toward healing is not simply about knowing ; it's about doing. It's an active process requiring intentional effort and real steps forward. Here's how I learned to care for myself in tough times.

Embracing Self-Care: Self-care gets a bad rap. People think it's all bubble baths and spa days. Real self-care, at its core, is more profound. It's the practice of recognizing and fulfilling what you need on every level: physical, mental, emotional, and spiritual.

Physical Self-Care: Physical self-care forms your foundation. Your body keeps score, remembering every stress, holding every tension. Sleep isn't lazy ; it's essential restoration. Nutritious food isn't just fuel ; it's medicine. Exercise isn't punishment ; it's a celebration of what your body can do. Regular check-ups aren't optional ; they're maintenance that keeps your foundation strong.

Try This: Set a gentle alarm three times today to pause, take three deep breaths, and stretch.

Mental Self-Care: Your mind needs tending like a garden, and that's where mental self-care comes in. Set firm boundaries with toxic people. Turn off notifications when you need quiet. Read books that feed your curiosity. Learn new skills at your own pace. Give yourself permission to say "no."

Step away from social media when it drains you. These walls protect your peace and create space for growth.

Try This: Choose one daily task (like washing dishes) and do it with complete focus - no phone, no TV, just presence.

Emotional Self-Care: Emotional self-care builds the rooms where you live with your feelings. Your emotions are messengers, not enemies. Journal your thoughts without censoring them. Cry when you need to because tears actually release stress hormones. Laugh often because it's literal medicine. Connect with people who get you. Feel your feelings without judgment. Seek therapy when you need support. Celebrate small wins. These rooms give you space to be human.

Try This: When a strong feeling arises today, name it without judgment: "Hello, anxiety, I see you're here."

Spiritual Self-Care: Spiritual self-care raises your roof toward something bigger than yourself. Meditate or pray regularly. Spend time in nature. Practice gratitude. Connect with your higher power, whatever that means to you. Find meaning in simple moments. Create a sacred space in your home. Honor your values through actions. This roof shelters your soul and gives meaning to everything below it.

Try This: Create a small sacred space somewhere in your home, even just a corner of your desk or windowsill.

Practicing Self-Care

Think of self-care like building a house. Physical care is the foundation, mental care forms the walls, emotional care creates the rooms, and spiritual care raises the roof. You need all parts working together to create a stable structure.

When you take care of yourself, you can show up better for everything and everyone else in your life. The following table will provide you with some ways to practice self-care and the practical reasons behind each method.

Ways to Practice Self-Care		
Tip	**How?**	**Why?**
Prioritize sleep	Stick to a bedtime routine, limit screens, and create a calming pre-sleep ritual.	For better mood and focus.
Enjoy hobbies	Dedicate time to activities you love to boost happiness.	To reduce stress and recharge.
Stay active	Choose enjoyable exercises like walking or dancing.	To improve health, mood, and sleep.
Practice mindfulness	Use daily meditation, yoga, or deep breathing.	To calm anxiety and support well-being.

Self-care is about making choices that honor your well-being in all areas of life. From sleep to movement, hobbies, and mindfulness, these practices help create a balanced, healthy lifestyle that nurtures both body and mind.

Consider how you speak to yourself when you make mistakes. Would you use those same words with a dear friend? What might change if you treated yourself with the same kindness you offer others?

Summing It Up

Eventually, I reached the point where I knew I had to forgive myself. Through prayer and consciously reframing those negative thoughts that surfaced about abortion, I reminded myself that nineteen-year-old me made the best choice she could with the information and resources she had.

I had to let go of my past to embrace my future. This didn't happen overnight. It came through small acts of self-compassion, through learning to be present with my pain instead of running from it, and through treating myself with the same grace I'd offer others.

Self-compassion and self-care are like two essential supports, both needed to lift you forward. Learning to shift from self-criticism to self-compassion is rarely straightforward. There will be days you feel light and free, making progress easily; other days, the weight of old habits may feel impossible to shake. But every attempt matters . Every gentle step forward counts.

For years, I carried the heavy burden of shame before I learned how to put it down. You don't have to wait that long. Begin today, even in the smallest way, and start from wherever you are. Trust that each small act of self-kindness has the power to create change.

Know this: Your worth is not defined by your mistakes; it's rooted in who you are. Healing is a gradual process, and that's completely okay. Self-care isn't a luxury or an indulgence—it's essential. You are worthy of your own kindness, no matter what. Every small, compassionate step you take matters more than you may realize.

Forgiving yourself can be one of the most difficult things you do, yet it opens up new paths and possibilities. Believe me, I've traveled this road.

And each step, though small, will guide you toward peace.

In our next chapter, we'll explore something that became crucial in my healing journey: developing a consistent spiritual practice. We'll talk about how connecting with something bigger than ourselves, whether through prayer, meditation, or your own unique path, can ground you when life feels chaotic. You'll learn how I found strength through faith during my darkest moments and how you can build your own spiritual foundation to support you through life's challenges.

Reflection Questions

1. How often do you take time to be fully present in the moment without distractions?

2. What are the signs that you need to slow down and practice more self-care?

3. In what ways do you speak to yourself when you make a mistake, and how can you show yourself more kindness?

4. How do you practice self-compassion when you're feeling overwhelmed or stressed?

5. What boundaries can you set to protect your time and energy for self-care and reflection?

16

Implementing and Maintaining Daily Spiritual Practice

"Faith is taking the first step even when you don't see the whole staircase."
-**Martin Luther King Jr.**

∞

Ten months into my paid internship at McAlester, Oklahoma, my world turned upside down with a single piece of paper. The sign on our classroom door read: "Computer labs are closed pending a scrub on all government-issued computers."

My stomach dropped. Just days before, two classmates had been fired for visiting porn sites on their work computers. Now, rumors flew through the halls like wildfire. Everyone wondered who might be next.

Then, the list appeared. Just initials, passed from hand to hand, supposedly naming those about to be fired. My heart stopped when I saw "M.P." Those were my initials.

Ten days. That's how long I lived in limbo between seeing my initials and being called into that conference room —ten days of barely eating, b arely sleeping, a nxiety eating me alive. The uncertainty crushed my chest like a weight.

But something shifted during those dark days. When panic threatened to overwhelm me, I found myself reaching for my Bible. When sleep wouldn't come, gospel music filled the silence. When fear gripped my throat, prayers tumbled out.

In those moments of uncertainty, standing outside that closed computer lab, I didn't yet understand how my spiritual foundation would become my lifeline. But before I tell you what happened next, let's explore why spiritual connection becomes crucial during life's storms.

Spirituality Theory

Spirituality isn't confined to church walls or meditation cushions. At its core, spirituality is about understanding and connecting with something bigger than ourselves, whether that's a higher power, the universe, or simply the deeper meaning of life. It focuses on how this connection can help us grow personally, find purpose, and improve our well-being.

Spiritual connection works on multiple levels:

1. Mental Clarity: Regular spiritual practice calms mental chaos. When your thoughts spin out of control, connecting with something bigger helps you step back and see the bigger picture.

2. Emotional Stability: Spirituality provides an emotional anchor. Those feelings of uncertainty, fear, and doubt? They don't disappear, but they lose their power to control you.

IMPLEMENTING AND MAINTAINING DAILY SPIRITUAL PRACTICE

3. Physical Impact: Your body responds to spiritual practice. Blood pressure drops. Stress hormones decrease. Even your immune system gets stronger.

4. Social Support: Spiritual communities offer real-world support. Whether it's a church group, meditation circle, or prayer partners, you're never truly alone.

When we talk about spirituality theory, we're really talking about how humans find meaning and purpose. According to the Pew Research Center, 42% of people use spiritual foundations to cope with stress. This means that they recover from setbacks faster and maintain hope even in dark times. Spirituality is an opportunity to root yourself in a vision far beyond your present surroundings, a calling that brings belonging.

When it comes to issues like low self-esteem, lack of confidence, or feeling out of control, spirituality can offer a path to healing and growth in a few different ways. The following table will lay it out for us.

How Spirituality Works			
Tip	How?	Why?	Examples
Building inner strength	Connecting with your spirituality can give you a sense of peace and assurance, knowing you're part of something larger.	This can boost self-esteem and confidence.	Starting each morning with prayer or meditation before you check your emails or social media

Encouraging self-reflection	Spiritual practices like meditation, prayer, or journaling encourage you to look within.	This helps you understand yourself better, face your fears, and develop self-control.	Journaling about your experiences and noting patterns in your reflections and choices
Providing perspective during challenges	Spirituality reminds you that challenges are a part of life and that they often carry lessons.	This mindset helps you approach obstacles with resilience instead of feeling defeated.	Reframing a job loss as an opening for a new direction
Fostering self-compassion	Spirituality encourages you to be kind to yourself, to forgive your mistakes, and to understand that personal growth is a journey.	These practices encourage patience with yourself and highlight that growth is a journey, not a destination.	Practicing forgiveness meditation when self-criticism arises

Spirituality acts as a guide, offering strength, clarity, and compassion when you need it most. Through consistent practices of self-reflection, viewing challenges as growth opportunities, and nurturing self-kindness, you can transform your approach to life's obstacles and find deeper fulfillment.

But these weren't just theories for me. As I faced those ten excruciating days between seeing my initials and learning my fate, every aspect of the spiritual connection I just described would be tested in real time.

When facing uncertainty, I found strength in scripture that spoke directly to my situation. Philippians 4:13 became my daily reminder: "I can do all things through Christ who strengthens me." These words became a lifeline, a promise I could hold onto when everything else felt unstable.

Ten Days That Tested Everything

There was a 10-day gap between hearing that my initials were on the list and the day I was finally called into the conference room by management. I was being terminated for misuse of the government computer. In those 10 days, I was an absolute wreck. I couldn't eat, I couldn't sleep, and my anxiety was through the roof. The uncertainty of it all weighed on me heavily. The only thing that brought me any sense of peace during that time was listening to gospel music, praying for strength, and reading my Bible for scriptures that reminded me of fortitude and resilience.

During those sleepless nights, 2 Corinthians 4:8-9 echoed in my mind: "We are hard pressed on every side, yet not crushed; we are perplexed, but not in despair; persecuted, but not forsaken; struck down, but not destroyed." These words perfectly captured my experience. While I felt pressed on every side by uncertainty, my faith assured me I wouldn't be crushed.

I leaned hard on my faith, something instilled in me from childhood that I knew would always be there in times of need. I also leaned into my friends, who were strong in their faith as well. They prayed with me and encouraged me with words that uplifted my spirit when I felt like

I was sinking. This experience tested my faith in a way that I had never encountered as an adult, but it also strengthened it. I realized that no matter how tough things got, my faith would carry me through.

Looking back, I see this as one of the pivotal moments in my life where I truly learned to rely on my faith and trust that God had a plan for me, even when it seemed like everything was falling apart. If God did it for me, I know He can do it for you too. You just have to trust in the process, lean into your faith, and know that you're never walking through challenges alone.

My experience during those ten days taught me that spiritual practice isn't just about finding peace ; it's about finding power. Let me show you how to build that power in your own life.

Building Your Spiritual Practice

Just like a muscle that needs consistent exercise to grow, spiritual strength flourishes with regular practice. Don't wait for a crisis to begin building your spiritual resilience; start laying the foundation now. Start small, but start today:

1. Morning Practice:
   - 5 minutes of silent meditation
   - Read one inspiring passage
   - Write 3 gratitudes
   - Set one clear intention

2. Throughout Your Day:
   - 3 deep breaths before meetings
   - Gratitude pause at lunch

- Brief walking meditation
- Listen to uplifting music

3. Evening Wind-Down:
   - Review the day's blessings
   - Release worry through prayer
   - Set tomorrow's intention
   - Peaceful visualization

As you begin building your own spiritual foundation, let Joshua 1:9 guide you: "Have I not commanded you? Be strong and of good courage; do not be afraid, nor be dismayed, for the Lord your God is with you wherever you go." This promise reminds us that we're never truly alone in our journey— whether we're starting a new practice or facing life's challenges, divine support is always with us.

But what happens when life throws you more than just daily stress? When a crisis hits, your spiritual practice becomes your lifeline. In my darkest moments, I discovered that doubling down on spiritual routines— not abandoning them— made all the difference. Even five minutes of focused prayer or meditation can anchor your day.

During those ten days of uncertainty in Oklahoma, I kept my Bible close, marking passages that spoke directly to my fears. I'd return to these words throughout the day, letting their wisdom sink deep into my spirit. Most importantly, I learned not to face challenges alone. My spiritual community became my strength. They prayed with me, reminded me of God's faithfulness, and held space for both my fears and my faith.

Take a moment to consider your own spiritual support system. Do you have people in your life who understand and nurture your spiritual growth?

If not, what steps could you take to begin building that community? Remember, spiritual connection doesn't always mean formal religious groups. It can be any gathering of people who share your values and support your journey toward deeper meaning and purpose.

Whether it's a prayer group, meditation circle, or trusted spiritual mentor, surrounding yourself with others who share your values creates a safety net when you feel like you're falling. The key isn't perfection in practice ; it's persistence. Show up for your spiritual routines even when life feels like it's spinning out of control. These practices form the foundation that will hold you steady through any storm.

Summing It Up

That morning in Oklahoma, when I saw my initials next to the word "disaster," the future seemed unclear, and I couldn't imagine a way forward. But in the midst of that crisis, my spiritual foundation held me up when everything else crumbled around me. Looking back now, I realize that losing that job wasn't an ending—it was the start of a new chapter, one where I learned to trust more deeply in the plan God had for me.

Your challenges may be different, and your spiritual journey may unfold in unique ways, but the core truth remains the same: when you've cultivated a strong spiritual foundation, you'll find the strength to weather any storm that comes your way.

The key is to start where you are. Commit to consistent practice, trust the process, and lean on the support of your faith community. Even when it's tough, continue showing up and trusting that growth is happening, even if you can't always see it right away.

As we close this chapter, know that your spiritual journey is just beginning. Every step you take in faith, every moment of prayer or reflection, and every choice to trust rather than fear is building something unbreakable within you.

Your past struggles do not dictate your future, and your present challenges are not the end of your story. With a solid spiritual foundation, you can face anything that lies ahead with grace, strength, and unwavering trust in God.

Remember, even in the darkest moments, there is light guiding your path. You are never alone on this journey. Keep moving forward, step by step, with faith leading the way.

Reflection Questions

1. How has your faith or spirituality helped you navigate challenging situations in your life?
2. When facing adversity, how do you lean into your spiritual beliefs to find strength and resilience?
3. What spiritual practices (prayer, meditation, reflection) do you engage in to nurture your inner peace and personal growth?
4. How has your spiritual journey shaped your understanding of yourself and your purpose in life?

17

The Power of Exploration

"I have often marveled at the thin line which separates success from failure."
-Ernest Shackleton

∞

As we wrap up our journey through the "Explore" section, I'm struck by how far we've all come. We began by elevating our thoughts, expanded our horizons, and finally, dove deep into exploring our authentic selves. Like that cross-country drive to California, every mile, even the hard ones, brought us closer to who we're meant to be.

Remember when we talked about my journey of forgiveness, about those twenty years of carrying guilt until I finally learned to show myself grace? That story, challenging as it was to share, taught us the power of self-compassion. We discovered that true healing is not passive. Rather, it demands active engagement with our pain and a deliberate choice to move toward growth.

Through stories of faith during my job loss in Oklahoma, we discovered that spiritual connection grounds us when everything else feels uncertain. We found that mindfulness can turn each moment into a growth opportunity, while self-care serves as a crucial foundation for both survival and thriving.

Key Concepts: The Pillars of "Explore"

Let's recap what we've learned in the "Explore" section:

1. Self-Compassion and Grace: We learned to treat ourselves with the same kindness we'd offer others.

2. Mind-Body-Spirit Connection: We discovered how aligning these three aspects creates true wellbeing.

3. Spiritual Foundation: We built practices that connect us to something greater than ourselves.

4. Authentic Self-Discovery: We found the courage to look within and embrace what we found.

Actionable Steps

So, what can you do to start expanding your life right now? Here are some actionable steps:

Putting "Explore" Into Practice	
Daily Spiritual Connection	Start each day with 5 minutes of prayer, meditation, or quiet reflection. Track how this centers you throughout your day.
Mind-Body-Spirit Alignment	Choose one activity daily that connects all three—like mindful walking, yoga, or sacred movement. Notice how your whole being responds.
Self-Compassion Practice	Set daily reminders to check in with yourself. When you notice self-criticism, pause and reframe it with kindness.

Putting "Explore" Into Practice	
Authentic Expression	Take time each week to express your true feelings through journaling, art, or conversation with trusted friends. Document your insights.
Inner Growth Review	Monthly, reflect on your journey. Note what practices resonate most, what challenges arose, and how you've grown.
Community Connection	Join or create a group that supports your spiritual growth. Share experiences and learn from others' journeys.
Sacred Self-Care	Designate specific times for activities that nourish your soul—whether that's reading spiritual texts, taking nature walks, or creating quiet space.
Growth Celebration	Weekly, acknowledge one way you've deepened your self-understanding. Share wins with your support system.

Exploring New Depths: What's Next?

This book may be ending, but your journey? It's just beginning. You've elevated your thinking beyond old limitations. You've expanded your horizons past comfortable boundaries. You've explored depths within yourself you maybe didn't know existed.

Think back to where we started. Remember those feelings of self-doubt? That inner critic that never seemed to quiet down? Through elevation, you learned to shift those thoughts. Through expansion, you proved those doubts wrong. Through exploration, you found your authentic voice.

Every tool we've discussed, from positive affirmations to mindfulness practices, from SMART goals to spiritual connection, now belongs to you. They're not just pages in a book but keys to continuing your growth.

The truth is, we never really stop exploring. Each day brings new opportunities to:

- Choose self-compassion over self-criticism
- Pick growth over comfort
- Select authenticity over approval
- Choose faith over fear

Your journey may have started with this book, but it extends far beyond these pages. You've built a foundation of self-awareness, developed tools for growth, and cultivated practices that will serve you for life.

Remember: You are stronger than you know, braver than you believe, and more capable than you imagine. You've proven this throughout our journey together. Now, it's time to take these lessons into your world and create the life you're meant to live.

Keep exploring. Keep growing. Keep believing in yourself.

Conclusion

∞

They used to call me the quiet one. The girl who didn't speak, who let her actions speak for her instead. The one who kept her head down, stayed in the background, and held her secrets close. That girl thought staying quiet was her shield, her protection from a world that felt too big, too overwhelming.

But life has a way of transforming us in the most unexpected ways.

Today, that same quiet girl has found her voice, and not just for herself. I've become a voice for the voiceless, a guide for those still finding their way through the shadows I once knew so well. Where I once struggled with extreme shyness and rock-bottom self-confidence, I now stand on stages, share my story, and empower other women to step into their power.

Remember when I told you about holding in my trauma for over twenty years? About how that six-year-old girl's experience shaped decades of silence? Now, instead of repressing my story, I share it openly, using my journey to light the way for others walking similar paths. Those very experiences that once felt like chains have become the keys to connecting with and uplifting others.

CONCLUSION

The transformation has been profound. Today, I'm not just surviving; I'm thriving and helping others do the same. Through the Triple E Podcast, I invite remarkable women to share their stories of resilience and growth. Each episode becomes a beacon of hope, showing others that they're not alone in their struggles and that transformation is possible.

The Triple E Tribe, my online community, has become a sanctuary for women in male-dominated industries. Here, we elevate mindsets, expand possibilities, and explore new horizons together. The same principles of growth that changed my life now serve as guideposts for others navigating their own journeys of transformation.

Perhaps most remarkably, through Soaring Without Limits Enterprises, I've found a way to help women literally expand their horizons. From the gleaming skyscrapers of Dubai to the serene shores of Bali, we create experiences that challenge comfort zones and ignite personal growth. These aren't just trips; they're transformational journeys that prove how far we can go when we dare to soar beyond our perceived limits.

Throughout this book, we've explored three powerful pathways to transformation. In Elevate, you've learned to raise your thought processes and redefine how you see yourself. Through overcoming thinking traps, embracing positive affirmations, and practicing gratitude, you've begun shifting your inner narrative. In Expand, you've been challenged to break free from self-imposed limitations, whether they stemmed from fear, doubt, or past experiences. And in Explore, you've discovered how to imagine and create new possibilities through self-care, spiritual practices, and consistent personal growth.

As you close these pages, I encourage you to take three important steps. First, review and complete the reflection questions at the end of each chapter, using them to create SMART goals for your next quarter, six months, and year ahead. Second, identify three key areas where you want to focus your growth and define the specific results you want to achieve. Finally, share this book with someone who could benefit from it, passing forward the tools and insights that resonated most with you.

This isn't meant to be a one-time read but a lifelong guide, one you can return to when you need inspiration, direction, or a gentle reminder that you have the power to create change. The tools, techniques, and strategies shared here are designed to support you through the highs and lows, the moments of self-doubt, and the moments of victory.

As you move forward, remember this: You are capable of more than you ever imagined. Every step, every shift in mindset, and every action you take brings you closer to the person you're meant to become. The life you desire is within reach. It's not about how quickly you get there ; it's about how dedicated you are to evolving and growing along the way.

So, keep soaring without limits.

Continue to elevate, expand, and explore.

And most importantly, trust in your journey, for it is uniquely yours. The best is yet to come.

Resources

Always A Lesson. (n.d.). How to be an effective accountability partner. Retrieved September 18, 2024, from https://alwaysalesson.com/how-to-be-an-effective-accountability-partner/

Armstrong, K. (2019, October 29). Carol Dweck on how growth mindsets can bear fruit in the classroom. APS-David Myers Distinguished Lecture on the Science and Craft of Teaching Psychological Science. https://www.psychologicalscience.org/observer/dweck-growth-mindsets

Bailey, R. R. (2019). Goal setting and action planning for health behavior change. American Journal of Lifestyle Medicine, 13(6), 615–618. https://doi.org/10.1177/1559827617729634

Bookey. (n.d.). Way of the Wolf by Jordan Belfort. Retrieved September 18, 2024, from https://www.bookey.app/quote-book/way-of-the-wolf-by-jordan-belfort

BrainyQuote. (n.d.). Alan Watts quote: "The more a thing tends to be permanent, the more it tends to be lifeless." Retrieved September 18, 2024, from https://www.brainyquote.com/quotes/alan_watts_386511

BrainyQuote. (n.d.). Neale Donald Walsch quote: "Life begins at the end of your comfort zone." Retrieved September 18, 2024, from https://www.brainyquote.com/quotes/neale_donald_walsch_452086

Cherry, K. (2024, May 9). How to boost your self-awareness: Here's why knowing yourself is so important—plus, how to improve it. Verywell Mind. https://www.verywellmind.com/what-is-self-awareness-2795023

Cherry, K. (2024, June 25). Self-efficacy and why believing in yourself matters. Verywell Mind. https://www.verywellmind.com/self-efficacy-and-why-believing-in-yourself-matters-4172351

Dakota Family Services. (n.d.). Thinking traps. Retrieved July 24, 2024, from https://dakotafamilyservices.org/resources/blog/archive/thinking-traps/

Duan, Y., Wang, J., Zhang, Z., & Li, W. (2019). Mindfulness-based interventions for individuals with attention deficit hyperactivity disorder (ADHD): A systematic review and meta-analysis. National Center for Biotechnology Information. Retrieved November 6, 2024, from https://pmc.ncbi.nlm.nih.gov/articles/PMC6480109/

Dweck, C. S. (2006). Mindset: The new psychology of success. Random House.

Falk, E. B., O'Donnell, M. B., Cascio, C. N., Tinney, F., Kang, Y., Lieberman, M. D., Taylor, S. E., An, L., Resnicow, K., & Stretcher, V. J. (2015). Self-affirmation alters the brain's response to health messages and subsequent behavior change. Proceedings of the National Academy of Sciences of the United States of America, 112(7), 1977–1982. https://doi.org/10.1073/pnas.1500247112

Gallup, Inc. (2024, November 6). Religion and wellbeing: An update. Gallup. Retrieved November 6, 2024, from https://news.gallup.com/opinion/polling-matters/389510/religion-wellbeing-update.aspx

RESOURCES

Goodreads. (n.d.). Success is not final, failure is not fatal: It is the courage to continue that counts. Retrieved September 18, 2024, from https://www.goodreads.com/quotes/3270-success-is-not-final-failure-is-not-fatal-it-is

Healyourrootswellness. (n.d.). Mindfulness and self-awareness: The keys to good mental health. Heal Your Roots Wellness. Retrieved November 6, 2024, from https://www.healyourrootswellness.com/blog/mindfulness-and-self-awareness-the-keys-to-good-mental-health

Huecker, M. R., Shreffler, J., McKeny, P. T., & Davis, D. (2023, July 31). Imposter phenomenon. In StatPearls. https://www.ncbi.nlm.nih.gov/books/NBK585058/

Hunter, B. (2018, August 23). Spanx's Sara Blakely: Embracing failure is the secret of her success. Foundation for Economic Education. https://fee.org/articles/spanx-s-sara-blakely-embracing-failure-is-the-secret-of-her-success/

Kroner, A. (2019, November 18). Mindfulness: The key to self-awareness. Brizo Magazine. Retrieved November 6, 2024, from https://brizomagazine.com/2019/11/18/mindfulness-the-key-to-self-awareness/

Lyra Health. (n.d.). Getting to know your thinking traps. Retrieved July 24, 2024, from https://www.lyrahealth.com/blog/getting-to-know-your-thinking-traps/

Mind Tools. (n.d.). Visualization: Using the power of your mind to achieve your goals. Retrieved September 18, 2024, from https://www.mindtools.com/a5ycdws/visualization

Moulton, M. (2023, September 30). Meditation: A path to self-awareness, personal growth, and a better workplace. LinkedIn. Retrieved November 6, 2024, from https://www.linkedin.com/pulse/meditation-path-self-awareness-personal-growth-better-mike/

Oxford English Dictionary. (n.d.). Impostor syndrome. In Oxford University Press. Retrieved September 1, 2024, from https://www.oed.com/dictionary/impostor-syndrome_n

Oxford Reference. (n.d.). Self-awareness. In Oxford University Press. Retrieved September 1, 2024, from https://www.oxfordreference.com/display/10.1093/oi/authority.20110803100453168

Pew Research Center. (2016, April 12). Religion in everyday life. Pew Research Center. Retrieved November 6, 2024, from https://www.pewresearch.org/religion/2016/04/12/religion-in-everyday-life/

Point Loma Nazarene University. (n.d.). What is impostor syndrome and how do I overcome it? Retrieved July 24, 2024, from https://www.pointloma.edu/resources/undergraduate-studies/what-impostor-syndrome-how-do-i-overcome-it

Pratt, M. (2022, February 17). The science of gratitude: Research shows gratitude isn't just a pleasant feeling—being grateful can also support greater health, happiness, and wisdom in ourselves and our communities. Mindful. https://www.mindful.org/the-science-of-gratitude/

Psychology, P. (n.d.). Resilience activities and exercises: 30 strategies to build resilience. Positive Psychology. Retrieved November 6, 2024, from https://positivepsychology.com/resilience-activities-exercises/

RESOURCES

Purdue Global. (2022, May 13). What are SMART goals? Updated January 2, 2024. https://www.purdueglobal.edu/blog/student-life/smart-goals-for-students/

ScienceDirect. (n.d.). Self-awareness. Retrieved July 24, 2024, from https://www.sciencedirect.com/topics/psychology/self-awareness

Stack Exchange. (2023, February 23). Where does this proverb come from: "If you want to go fast, go alone; if you want to go far, go together". English Language & Usage. https://english.stackexchange.com/questions/606293/where-does-this-proverb-come-from-if-you-want-to-go-fast-go-alone-if-you-wan

Study.com. (n.d.). Self-introspection & self-awareness theory: Overview & examples. Retrieved July 24, 2024, from https://study.com/learn/lesson/self-introspection-self-awareness-theory-overview-examples.html

Success Starts Within. (n.d.). Visualization techniques for athletes. Retrieved September 18, 2024, from https://www.successstartswithin.com/sports-psychology-articles/visualization-for-sports/visualization-techniques-for-athletes/

The Good Trade. (n.d.). Cultivating spirituality. The Good Trade. Retrieved November 6, 2024, from https://www.thegoodtrade.com/features/cultivating-spirituality/

University of Utah Health. (2021, November). Practicing gratitude for better health and well-being. HealthFeed. https://healthcare.utah.edu/healthfeed/2021/11/practicing-gratitude-better-health-and-well-being

Villarreal, A. A. (2023, May 13). Mindset: The new psychology of success. LinkedIn. https://www.linkedin.com/pulse/mindset-new-psychology-success-aldo-a-villarreal-s/

White, D. B. (n.d.). Managing stress & discovering self-awareness with mindfulness. Awakened Path Counseling. Retrieved November 6, 2024, from https://www.awakenedpathcounseling.com/manage-stress-with-mindfulness/